# Murder in Lakeview

Enjoy
Terry

*Terry F. Simpson*

# Disclaimer

Although this is a work of fiction, the places mentioned are real,
only the characters are the imagination of the author.
The opinions expressed in this book are solely the opinions
of the author, and do not represent the opinions of the publisher.
The author has represented and warranted full ownership
and/or legal right to publish all the material in this book.

# Acknowledgements

A special thanks to Gretchen Martelle
for her editing and encouragement.
You are truly a great friend.

To Samantha K. Cook
for the art work that truly brings my book to life.

# Dedication

This book is dedicated to my loving wife Jenifer:
she is my proofreader, my moral supporter, and
understanding partner.

Thank you for your wisdom and support.

Without your love and encouragement
this work wouldn't have been completed.

# Murder in Lakeview

*Chapter One*

onday morning, June 4, 2012. The services for Annie Marie Blake are heard in a small funeral home in the Village of Adams, New York. A red-eyed husband, Tom, gave an emotional eulogy. He spoke of Annie, his wife, partner in life, and unconditional friend. Taken before their dreams and accomplishments could be completed.

Annie Marie Blake -- born May 17, 1952, the only daughter of John and Marie Asland of Evans, Georgia. Annie graduated from Greenbrier High School in Evans in 1970, and earned a bachelor's degree in math at The North Country Community College in Saranac Lake, New York. There she developed a strong love for the Adirondack Mountains. Annie completed her Masters Degree in Education at Oswego State University. She then worked as a kindergarten teacher at the Wilson Elementary Building of the South Jefferson School District in Adams Center, New York.

In her adult years Annie stood about five foot two inches and tipped the scales at one hundred ten pounds. She had reddish blond curly hair and green eyes. Annie always wore a smile on her face. Her parents both passed away at an early age of heart disease.

Thomas William Blake was born on April 11, 1952, the only son of William and Rosemary Blake. Tom also graduated from Greenbrier High School in Evans, Georgia. After graduation he enlisted in the Navy and completed his basic training at the RTC (Recruit Training Center) on the Great Lakes at Chicago, Illinois. After basic he completed his advanced individual training in California. From there Tom deployed to the Philippines where he spent the remainder of his Navy career building schools for the local population. Tom stood six foot tall and weighed in at one hundred eighty five pounds. His eyes were a beautiful blue. Tom kept his dark hair neatly combed and was always clean shaven.

The congregation listened quietly as Tom choked back tears. In the front row sat Tom's employer, David Willard. Next to him sat Annie's boss, Joann Richards, from the elementary school. Tom's mother Rosemary Blake sat front row center with Kleenex in hand, continuously drying her eyes. Robert and Donna Thompson, neighbors and closest friends of Annie and Tom completed the front row. Bob is a representative of an automobile franchise and spends a lot of his time on the road, often out of the country. A secretary in the office, Donna worked at the same school Annie did. Annie and Donna shared many lunches together and solved the world's problems over coffee.

When the service ended the congregation all passed by Annie's portrait and urn to console Tom with a hand shake, a hug, and a few kind words. David Willard told Tom to take all the time he needed. Joann Richards said Annie was the most wonderful teacher she had ever known. She would be hard to replace. Tom's mother Rosemary, quite frail and in a wheel chair, pulled Tom down to her and gave him a kiss on the cheek as tears caressed her face. With a heartfelt hug for her son, Rosemary was choked with emotion and unable to speak. Bob Thompson shook his hand and gave Tom a back-slapping hug and said, "Don't be a stranger. We're right next door." Tom nodded his thanks. Donna Thompson too was filled with emotion as she held Tom as tightly as she could. She choked back her tears and searched for the words that would express the sadness she felt. She was only able to say, "If you need anything, anything at all, don't be afraid to ask. We love you guys, okay? I mean it Tom. We're there for you." Donna was the last to speak with Tom. Everyone else had left to gather at the local American Legion, Don Rounds Post 586, for a small luncheon.

At the Legion a collage of pictures of Annie was beside the buffet table. There Tom stood and spoke to everyone that passed and answered questions about any of the pictures in the collage. Most were of camping trips in the Adirondacks, some were pictures taken at work. A few were of family, most already passed.

Donna and Bob were sitting at a table away from the crowd, quietly talking to each other. Donna noticed a young lady holding Tom's arm as she stood on her tiptoes and gave Tom a kiss on the cheek. Tom was almost unresponsive to the kiss, which took Donna by surprise. She leaned over to Bob and asked, "Who is the young woman with Tom?"

Bob looked to the left and right of Tom and said, "What woman?"

Looking back, Donna responded, "I don't see her now. She was just there."

The luncheon slowly cleared out. Tom grabbed a garbage can to start picking up. Bob and Donna jumped right in and together they quickly had the post back in order. Tom thanked the staff at the post for everything, shook Bob's hand and gave Donna another hug.

Donna asked, "Tom, who was the young woman that gave you a kiss by the collage?"

Tom looked puzzled and said, "I don't know. I really don't remember any kiss. But it's been a very emotional day for me today. I probably just didn't notice. Again, thank you. I think it's time for me to just go home. I don't think I have slept since Annie died. Hopefully I'll get some much needed sleep."

Tom grabbed the collage of pictures and walked out the door to his truck. From there he drove back to Adams Center, to a much-too-quiet house, cold without his wonderful Annie.

# Memories

## Chapter Two

Tom was completely exhausted. He sat in his chair and just stared at the ceiling. It was easy to cry and he did. He tried to eat, just a cold sandwich or a bowl of cereal, anything easy. Nothing he tried tasted good. He was sure he didn't want to cook. After a while his eyes closed and sleep came. It was a wonderful sleep. As soon as he closed his eyes he saw Annie back in high school. A sandy-haired girl with a big smile, Annie always wore a pair of jeans with a sweatshirt or loosely fitting blouse. She was always a country girl. She played softball and was a long-time member of the Girl Scouts. Camping was an endless adventure. There was always a new place to go -- a canoe trip she hadn't paddled, a mountain she hadn't climbed or a trail she hadn't hiked. That's what brought her to Saranac Lake to college, the allure of the Adirondack Mountains. There she could be Annie.

Tom and Annie dated in high school. After school they both had dreams and ambitions and a serious relationship was not going to interfere with any of it. Annie wanted to be a teacher and if possible a kindergarten teacher. She loved the little kids. They always made her smile. Annie had a way about her. Any child that was shy or withdrawn soon came out of their shell by just being with Annie.

After Tom was discharged from the Navy he didn't look for a job right away so he decided to go north to see Annie. She was glad he did. They dated and discussed their next move. It was decided that Annie would apply for teaching jobs in hopes of getting a job somewhere near the Adirondacks. She hoped to be teaching the little kids. Tom figured he could get a job just about anywhere with his construction background.

Annie mailed out résumés to schools all over New York State. With her 4.0 average in college and an outstanding score from her student teaching, she received twelve requests for interviews. Adamant about what she wanted to do, she received three offers. Annie became the kindergarten teacher at the Wilson Elementary Building of the South Jefferson Central School District.

Tom and Annie moved to the small town of Adams Center, where they rented a house just outside of town on Kellogg Hill. They didn't have much so it didn't take long to settle in. There was so much to do. School was to start in just two weeks. It was important to get everything in place for Annie. They made several trips to the school to check on her room and supplies. They made some purchases to make it warm for the kids' first time away from mommy. Next they went to the local department store for the proper attire for a brand new kindergarten teacher. The glow on Annie's face that first day of school was priceless. No words could explain the joy in Annie's heart. That joy never left. She truly loved teaching.

After Annie was settled in, Tom started looking for a job. Most contractors were willing to give him a shot, but jobs were small and came with no guarantee that they would keep him on through the winter. Tom finally decided to work for North Country Builders. *"I've got to start somewhere,"* he thought.

They quickly fell into a routine. Tom picked up quickly on how the new boss liked to have things done and was continually able to please him. It was not long until he was going out alone on small jobs, doing whatever needed to be done. Tom never had a complaint from any customer about the work he did. Soon he was making good money and was assured of work through the winter.

Annie, in her first year, constantly presented new ideas to her supervisor of ways to make learning fun and exciting for the children: new games to play, riddles to learn to help the children learn the basics of the alphabet, their names, addresses, and phone numbers and other information each child needed to learn and continue to developed and grow, each in their own way.

The demands of a new job, new challenges and everyday stress began to level out at the completion of Annie's first year in school. Summer vacation was upon them. Tom had earned his first two-week vacation. They could finally think of something more than just work.

It was Saturday morning, their first day of vacation. Tom got up early, made coffee and dug out a few pamphlets of attractions in the Adirondacks he had picked up over the last year. He took everything outside and placed it on their picnic table, a carafe of coffee, cream, sugar, two blueberry muffins and the pamphlets. Tom then gingerly trotted upstairs, tore back the covers from Annie and scooped her up in his arms. With a slight giggle Annie put her arms around Tom's neck and said with a smile, "What are you doing?"

"I'm taking you on vacation, anywhere you want to go." With that he carried Annie downstairs, out the back door and gently set her down at the picnic table.

"Coffee, madam?"

"Why yes Tom, please."

"Cream? Sugar? Oh, I picked up a couple of blueberry muffins. I forgot the butter. Would you like some butter?"

"No, silly, sit down! Oh my god, this is wonderful! Just what do you have up your sleeve anyway?"

Tom poured himself a cup of black coffee and sat down next to Annie.

"Over the past year I have picked up a few pamphlets of some attractions in your beloved Adirondacks. I would love to take you there, up there, anywhere. That is, if you haven't already been there, you know, up there." Tom tilted his head to one side and said in a shy little voice, "Anywhere?" Annie held her chin in her right hand, looked to her left at Tom and giggled.

"Oh my god Tom," Annie laughed. "You are a dream come true. I love you. Please don't ever change."

"I have no intention of ever being anything but in love with you Annie."

Annie gave a loving sigh as Tom gave her a loving kiss.

"Okay Tom, let's see what you've got. High Falls Gorge, 1000 Animals, Natural Bridge and Caverns. Oh, here's one, Santa's Workshop. Whiteface Mountain Memorial Highway. Whiteface Mountain Aerial Chairlift, Frontier Town!" With a scowl on her face she read, "*Where you'll ride a train through the wilderness and be held up by bandits, or chased to Fort Apache by renegade Indians.* Oh Tom, I have a much better idea. Let's just go camping. We can buy a tent and a couple of sleeping bags and disappear into the hills like wanted bandits. Right after we rob the Wells Fargo Stage."

Tom and Annie laughed and gave each other a high five.

"You've got yourself a deal Annie!"

Her coffee and muffin gone, Annie stood up from the table, "I have to take a shower and get dressed and then we can go shopping!"

"Yeah, me too, I'll join you. It would be faster if we took one together."

With a shy grin on her face Annie responded, "Oh you bad boy. What have you got on your mind now?"

Tom jumped to his feet. Annie, with a laughing little scream, turned and ran for the house.

# First day after the funeral
## Chapter Three

Tom woke up early at 5 a.m., his normal time to arise. He went to the kitchen and made a pot of coffee. With coffee in hand he sat down at the table and just stared out the window. *"I need to weed Annie's flower garden. She wouldn't like a single weed in it,"* he thought. Tom managed to fix himself two slices of wheat toast with just butter. *"Come on, Tom,"* he thought, *"get your butt in gear. Put on your sneakers, shorts and T-shirt and go for your morning constitutional. Let's start the day out right."* Tom finished his breakfast and was soon out the door.

He ran his usual five miles with thoughts back to when he started running for Annie. That was what she wanted, so he, like some men anyway, did almost whatever she wanted.

Standing at her kitchen sink, Donna Thompson saw Tom return from his morning run. He jogged up the front steps, turned and sat down on the front porch swing. *Right beside that young woman*, the same woman that gave him the kiss at Annie's reception. Who is she? Donna turned and called to Bob, "Would you come down here? You've got to see this!"

Bob came into the kitchen with a worried look on his face.

"What's wrong?"

"It's that young woman! The one who gave Tom the kiss at the reception. She is sitting in the swing with Tom on his front porch. Who is she?"

Bob looked out the window just as Tom walked into the house.

"He just went inside Donna. I don't see anybody else."

"She must have gone in ahead of him. I really wonder who she is Bob. You don't suppose something has been going on, do you?"

"No! You're starting to imagine things. Tom absolutely loved Annie. He wouldn't cheat on her. Not ever, no way, no how."

"Well something is going on. Annie was my best friend and I'm going to keep my eye out."

Bob finished his breakfast, gave Donna a kiss and headed for work. As he walked to his car, Tom came out the front door.

"Good morning Tom. How is everything this morning?"

"Oh you know Bob, got to keep myself busy. I'm going to weed Annie's garden this morning. I really don't feel much like going to work."

"Well, I think it's important to keep your mind busy. You know, don't dwell on what has just happened. That won't do you any good. I suggest you go back to work as soon as you can, Tom."

"Okay, thanks Bob. I'll think about it."

Tom got the gardening tools out of the garage, got down on his knees and began fiddling around in Annie's garden. There wasn't much to do. She always tried to keep her garden weed free.

Donna, back at her kitchen window, saw Tom on his knees, weeding the garden. Standing on the porch, leaning against the post, drinking her coffee and watching him, was the young woman. When Donna looked again she was gone. *"Just who is she? She sure appears to be making herself at home. I don't care what Bob thinks, I'm really curious,"* Donna thought.

Tom worked in the garden for a while and became very tired. "Wow, I need a nap," he said to himself. Tom got off his knees, wandered up the porch steps and into the house. His favorite chair was beckoning to him to sit down and he was soon asleep.

# The Department Store
## Chapter Four

Tom stretched in his chair with a big sigh. "What time is it?" he wondered. Looking at the grandfather clock in the corner, it was just 12:30 pm. "Wow, I knew I was tired, but 12:30 tired? That's got to be a record," Tom marveled.

Tom went to the kitchen and grabbed a bottle of water from the fridge. Food was just not on his mind. He downed a couple healthy gulps of his water, he then went to the bathroom to take a much needed shower. With a smile on his face, he remembered the playful sex they had that morning so many years ago. He striped her naked in the bathroom, caressed her body in the shower and rolled around endlessly under the sheets. Completely wiped out, they dozed off to sleep.

Annie woke up shortly after noon and rolled out of bed. She noticed the time, grabbed the sheets and yanked them off Tom.

"Get up lazy boy! If you're going to take me camping, we need to go shopping so get up!"

Tom sat up on the edge of the bed, grabbed his pants and pulled them up to his knees. He then stood up and pulled them over his hips. They finished the task of making themselves presentable in the public's eye, grabbed the truck keys and walked out the door.

Annie, starving right to death, asked Tom to stop at Lillie's, the local dinner, for a quick bite. As they entered, Lillie, behind the counter, gave them a warm greeting.

"Tom, Annie how are you two?"

"We're good, how about you?"

"Great! Coffee?"

"Please," Annie responded. Lillie grabbed the coffee and a couple of menus and placed them on their table.

"What are you two doing today?"

"Tom is taking me camping for our vacation and we need to buy a few things: tent, sleeping bags, you know, pretty much everything," Annie said with a big smile.

Annie ordered a BLT on wheat with a few chips.

"That sounds good Lilly, I'll have the same."

"Coming right up. Order," Lillie shouted in the kitchen. Tom and Annie finished lunch, paid the tab and waved to Lillie as they left. Lillie shouted, "Have fun, you two!"

At the department store they picked out a lightweight two-man tent, two ultra light 30 degree sleeping bags, two external frame back packs, water purifier, pack stove and a couple water bottles.

"What are we going to eat Annie?"

"We'll pick up some freeze dried food at an outdoor store near Star Lake."

"Freeze dried, isn't that kind of blah-tasting stuff?"

Annie laughed, "You'll be surprised, I'm sure. It's really good."

They returned home, packed a few things and were soon on the road heading North through Carthage, Natural Bridge, and Harrisville. Approaching Star Lake, they stopped at the Outdoor Emporium. Annie picked up some chili-mac, beef stew, scrambled eggs, and some chicken teriyaki.

"We need a couple of coffee cups too Tom, and grab a jar of instant coffee."

"What about plates Annie?"

"We'll eat it right out of the bag." They paid the tab and again hit the road.

Annie took the reins for the short drive through the small village of Star Lake. Tom's attention was fixed out his side window. This was his first time inside the Blue Line. They traveled East on State Route 3 until Annie slowed and turned on her right hand signal. "This is where we turn." The bill board read, *Wanakena*.

"Have you been here before Annie?"

"Some of my friends from college and I came here a few times. There are some great trails here with a difficulty rating of easy. I figured this would be a good place for you to start on your very first experience. I really want you to enjoy this."

They pulled up in front of the General Store and parked the truck.

"Is this where we start Annie?"

"Not really. I want to show you the famous Wanakena foot bridge. Back when this was a logging, town the workers crossed this bridge every day to get to the mill. It's now on the National Register of historic places.

Together they walked to the bridge. A smiling Tom almost yelled. "Wow, this is cool!"

"The Adirondacks are full of amazing places, Tom."

"Ok, I'm impressed already, and I'm sure you have plenty more to show me."

With a big smile on Annie's face, "Count on it!" They entered the store just to pick up a couple of sodas and a candy bar. "This will give you an energy boost, Tom. I'm sure you don't need it but, it will be your last for about a week. So if you want to back out, this is your last chance."

"Hell no, you've got me intrigued. I'm ready to go!"

Annie drove to the trail head and parked the truck.

"First things first Tom, We must sign in at the trail register, that box over there." She opened the box and explained to Tom that if a hiker is gone too long and people become concerned about your safety, this is where the forest rangers begin to look.

"Several places along the trail there are these sign-in boxes. If you signed in here and not at the next box, it gives them a place to start looking."

"How clever is that?"

Tom helped Annie with her thirty eight pound pack, and Annie held Tom's until he managed to shoulder the straps and draw tight the hip belt. "Now clip the chest strap to hold your shoulder straps in place. You're carrying forty-two pounds Tom! How does it feel?"

"Not bad. The weight seems to be all on my hips."

"Okay, that's a good start. I plan a short walk today. If Janecks Landing is empty we'll stay there tonight."

"Any idea how far that is?"

"Not far Tom, about three and a half miles on mostly old railroad bed. We should get going. We don't have a whole lot of time before it will start to get dark."

They started up the trail with two of the biggest smiles -- a new adventure for Tom and one of Annie's greatest loves, experiencing nature in the Adirondack Park.

The trail was wide enough they could walk side by side holding each other's hand. Tom and Annie talked and laughed all the way to the end of the railroad bed. Annie then took the lead.

"We'll walk around the end of Dead Creek flow over to Janecks Landing. If no one is there we'll make camp Tom."

"Sounds good to me!"

They continued on as the trail was more like a traditional trail: much narrower, wet in many places, through a dense forest.

As they arrived at the lean-to an enthusiastic Annie stated, "We're in luck Tom, It's empty. We'll stay here tonight." She slid her backpack to the ground and placed it in the lean-to. Tom followed her lead and slid out of his.

"How do you feel Tom?"

"A lot lighter right now," he laughed. "It may be hard to keep my feet on the ground; other than that, no problem."

"Good, you may work out yet. So keep it up."

"I'm putting my best foot forward, one step at a time Annie."

Annie grabbed Tom's hand and together they walked to the shore.

"Beautiful, isn't it Tom?"

"Wow, it's nothing like downtown that's for sure. You know, I haven't seen anyone since we left the Truck. Is it always like this?"

"Not always. It depends on where you go. Some areas are more popular than others."

"Can we swim here Annie?"

"I don't know why not."

"Good, I'm a little sweaty from the hike. I'll grab my suit. Going to join me?"

"Sounds good," Annie stated as they raced to the lean-to.

With his suit on, Tom ran to the water, slowed to a walk and made a shallow dive on the surface of the water. He rolled over on his back, stood up and gasped for air.

"Holy crap, that's cold!"

Annie, a little more cautious, walked in up to her hips and slowly dove in and swam over to Tom. She stood up, put her arms around him and said, "Here, let me warm you up," as she placed a passionate kiss on his lips. "Any better?"

"A little," he said, "but I'm still very cold," and he kissed her again. Tom held her tight for several minutes. "I love you Annie."

She looked him in his beautiful blue eyes. "I love you too Tom."

Hand in hand they left the water and walked back to the lean-to. As they were changing their clothes Annie said, "Put on your clean dry sweats for around camp Tom. We'll wear the light-weight shirts and nylon pants we wore in today, again tomorrow while we are on the trail."

"That makes sense."

Tom and Annie spent a little time opening up their sleeping bags and hanging them in the lean-to, along with hanging their swim suits and towels from the roof at each side of the lean-to. Hopefully to dry before packing them up tomorrow.

"I don't know about you Tom, but I could use a cup of coffee."

"Yeah, that's sounds good."

"Take the pot and go to the lake and get some water. It has to boil for three minutes before we can drink it. We'll make our coffee with that and use our water purifier for our drinking water on the trail tomorrow."

"Got it."

As they drank their coffee Tom and Annie just sat in the lean-to and talked. They talked about after the house and the white picket fence. What was their plan? Tom spoke of his work. He liked his present boss but really wanted to get in with a bigger company, working on developments, housing complexes, schools and office buildings.

"I'm sure the money would be union scale, and maybe I could even join a union. I really would like some provided benefits, especially a retirement plan. Hopefully I'll be able to retire someday. I really don't want to work till the day I die."

Annie spoke of school. "I really love my job, the kids and the people I work with. Really Tom, I have it all: job, benefits, retirement. And you know what? I'm the luckiest girl in the world. I have you. It just doesn't get any better than that."

Tom smiled and gave a little laugh.

"As long as we're together Annie, I don't really care where I work."

Annie put water on to boil for dinner. Tom started working on gathering wood for a bonfire. Annie soon joined him. Some pieces were too long so Tom tried to smash them on the ground to break them in half, which didn't work very well.

"I'll show you a little trick Tom. Just find a couple of trees close together. Put the limb between them and bend the limb around the tree. If that doesn't work, use my banana saw. It cuts on the pull stroke. But be careful. It's very sharp."

Tom took her lead and Together they gathered plenty of wood for the night.

Standing next to the fire pit, Tom looked a little puzzled.

"I'm not even going to try Annie. How do you start a fire?"

"Old woodsman's trick. Take this piece of candle, place it in the bottom of the fire pit and light it. Then start sprinkling pine needles over the flame. When they are burning good start putting on small twigs, then use bigger ones until you have a fire."

"Okay, I can do this." And he did.

With a nice campfire burning, Annie handed Tom his first freeze dried meal, beef stew. Tom took a spoonful and gasped for air.

"Wow, that's hot!" As he waved his hand in front of his mouth.

Annie laughed and said, "Well blow on it, silly. His next spoonful was much better.

"M-m-m! That is good! What's for dessert?"

"Well, we have some chocolate chip cookies Tom, but only two or they won't last the week."

After another cup of coffee Tom and Annie just sat at the edge of the lean-to. Annie held Tom's arm and placed her head on his shoulder and, without saying a word, they just watched the fire for hours.

# Their First Climb
## Chapter Five

Morning came and Tom woke up flat on his back with Annie's head on his shoulder. He didn't move, just listened to the quiet. Soon, Mother Nature started her call and Tom had to get up. He tried to gently slide his shoulder out from under Annie's head without waking her up, but that didn't work. Annie moaned, "Oh don't leave. I was so comfortable."

"Sorry. Mother Nature is calling." He slid out of his sleeping bag, pulled on a pair of shoes and stepped out of sight.

Annie remained in the sack, just looking at their smoldering fire. When Tom returned she asked him to make the coffee.

"It will be my pleasure."

Tom pulled out the pack stove, grabbed the pot and went to the lake for water. He stood on the shore and gasped in awe at the scene that lay before him. Calm waters, so calm it was a mirror image of the opposite shore line. A fog rising off the water was the most beautiful thing he had ever seen. Tom just stood there, unable to move.

Annie walked up behind him. "Beautiful isn't it?"

Tom turned his head, smiled at Annie, then turned back to the scene. "It's the most beautiful thing I think I have ever seen. I just don't have any words to describe it."

Tom finally bent over and filled the pot with water, turned and started back toward camp. Annie grabbed Tom's arm and placed her head on his shoulder as they walked back.

"I started the pack stove, Tom. I thought you would be right back."

"I would have, but I was caught up in the moment, I guess."

Annie smiled, "I know. Sometimes I still get emotional at what I see up here."

"Would you like me to fix the fire Annie?"

"I'm not cold Tom, Just relax, the coffee will be hot in just a minute. Then I'll fix us some breakfast."

"Sounds like a plan." The coffee was soon hot and Annie fixed the freeze-dried scrambled eggs. After breakfast, as they were sipping on their coffee, Annie asked Tom how he slept.

"I slept well, but that floor leaves something to be desired."

Annie laughed. "I'll take care of that tonight, we'll sleep on the ground in our tent."

"Okay, we'll give that a try."

They finished their coffee and began packing up.

"Before we pack away the pot, would you go to the lake and get some water for the fire to be sure it's out, Tom?"

"Sure, Good idea."

They finished packing up, donned their packs and again hit the trail. At their first junction, there was another sign-in box. After registering they closed the box and headed for Glasby Pond. A short distance up the trail they came across another junction, to the right, the trail leads to High Falls.

"We'll take that trail on our way back Tom. We're going this way today," and they continued on straight ahead.

About an hour on up the trail Tom paused. "Is that water I hear running?"

"Yes it is. It's the outlet from Glasby Pond. We're almost there."

"Wow, that didn't take long."

They walked in front of the beaver dam at the end of the pond and Annie pointed, "That's Glasby. They tell me the fishing is pretty good here in the spring. The camp site is just up here a little further." Just ahead the camp site was on the right side of the trail. Tom and Annie slipped out of their backpacks and leaned them against a tree.

"What now Annie? Possibly a drink or two of my water would be good. I am thirsty."

"I'm sorry Tom, I should have ask if you needed a break."

Tom took a couple good slugs and wiped the sweat from his forehead. "I'm good, what's next?"

"I think we should set up our tent Tom so if anyone else comes along they will know this site is taken."

"Okay," Tom took the tent off his backpack. Since the tent was brand new, Annie grabbed the instructions and read them. Step one, Step two, and so on. Soon, tent with rain fly were proudly sitting in the middle of the campsite, about ten yards behind the fire pit.

"Looks good Annie. I'll start gathering some firewood."

"Okay, I'll unpack our sleeping bags."

Tom gathered a nice pile of wood, broke some, cut some and gathered some pine needles and twigs to get the fire started. There was no lean-to here so they just sat on the ground with their backs against a tree.

"What do you have in mind for the rest of the day, Annie?"

"Well, I thought we could have lunch on top of Cat Mountain. What do you think?"

"I'm game, let's do it!"

Feeling refreshed they grabbed their water bottles and the bag of cookies and headed up the trail. It wasn't far to the junction to Cat Mountain. From there it was seven-tenths of a mile to the top. Tom had to stop several times going up. With his hands in his hips, taking a deep breath he said, "Whew, I'm not used to this."

Annie just smiled. "This is nothing. Wait till you try the High Peaks."

"High Peaks, huh? I'm having trouble in the foothills," Tom took another deep breath, then forced his legs upward.

He waved Annie onward. The last section was the steepest and when they broke out into the open at the summit, Tom held his knees and gasped for air.

"Oh man, I'm out of shape for this kind of stuff."

"You know, Tom that it's only a four hundred foot change in elevation from where we stayed last night. Janecks, the man the landing was named after, was the forest ranger who manned the fire tower that was here on Cat Mountain. He walked that trail every day, on one leg. He lost the other in a logging accident.

"You're shitting me!"

"Nope, God's honest truth."

"Now I know I'm out of shape. I'll get better, I promise."

Sitting at the top, they enjoyed a beautiful blue sky with those white puffy clouds, a warm sun shining down on them and a vast forest lying at their feet.

"Holy crap Annie! This is beautiful. I just can't believe it!"

They sat near the edge, had a drink of water and shared the cookies.

"You want to know something, Tom?"

"Sure. What?"

"There are forty-six high peaks in the Adirondack Park. If you climb all forty-six you become what is known as a Forty-Sixer. And Tom. I would like to become a Forty-Sixer. What do you think, will you do it with me?"

"I think I'll have to get into shape, that's what I think. And I wouldn't want to do it with anyone else. You know Annie, we can make this our destination every summer. How long do you think it will take?"

"It can take as long as we want. I prefer to enjoy the journey as well as the destination." Annie held up her hand, looked Tom in the eye and nodded her head. "Deal?"

Tom gave her a high five and said smiling, "Deal!"

Tom and Annie talked more about their destination and just how to get there. Each summer they would spend as much time in the mountains as possible and climb as many mountains as time would allow. Perhaps they would climb ten, or maybe just one. As Annie said, enjoy the journey not just the destination.

They wandered back down the mountain to Glasby Pond as late afternoon approached. Back at camp, Tom started working on the bonfire and Annie prepared dinner.

"How about chili-mac tonight Tom?"

"Sounds good to me."

It wasn't long until they were putting away another surprisingly good-tasting freeze-dried meal.

"I can't believe this stuff Annie, It's really good."

"I'm glad you like it because it sounds like we'll be eating a lot of it."

After dinner Annie made another cup of coffee for both of them and they each ate two more cookies. Their conversation drifted back to what they wanted out of life besides the house with the white picket fence. Tom asked if she wanted children. Annie response was. "Oh yes, you know that I love children. I'm not saying that I want a dozen, or just one. I will have whatever God gives me, when God gives them to me. But I'm not in any hurry either. How about you, Tom? Do you want children?"

"I'll be perfectly honest with you Annie, I haven't really thought about it. I guess my comment is, what will be will be." Annie smiled and just laid her head on Tom's shoulder.

They sat watching the fire and talking for hours, while in the distance a loon made his lonely call.

"Did you hear that, Annie?"

"Oh yes. Beautiful, isn't it? It's a loon, probably calling to his mate, but don't quote me on that. I really don't know what he's saying. All I know is that it's beautiful."

"I won't disagree with you."

In the morning, Tom again got up and made coffee while Annie slept in. He took his first cup to the pond's edge and watched as the loon made small ripples in the dead calm water, a slight mist gently lifting from the surface. *"I don't think this will ever get old,"* he thought. After a bit, Tom heard Annie stirring back at camp. He wandered back and made her first cup of coffee.

"Thank you. How did you sleep last night, Tom?"

"Believe it or not, I slept better on the ground than I did on that wooden floor." With her hair in her face, Annie looked at Tom, blew the hair out of her eyes and smiled.

"Good. The air is so fresh out here I always sleep good, anywhere -- on the ground, on the floor, or on a pack mattress."

"What do you have in mind for today Annie?"

"I thought we could go over to Cow Horn Pond. We have to go past the junction to Cat Mountain, then past Cat Mountain Pond, then to another junction. One way heads for Lowe's Lake. The other way heads for The West Flow. We'll go that way, then turn off that trail and go down to Cow Horn Pond. There's a lean-to there but we can pitch our tent to sleep in if you want Tom."

"Whatever works is fine with me.

They finished their second cup of coffee and started the task of packing up. Before Tom packed the pot, he went to the pond for some water to be sure the fire was out. He packed the pot away, then grabbed Annie's pack and lifted it onto her back. Annie slipped her arms under the shoulder straps and clipped her hip belt. With the pack resting comfortably on her hips, she clipped her chest strap.

"It's good. Thanks Tom."

Tom placed his on a stump, slipped his right arm under the strap, then his left and hoisted his pack to his back.

"Here, let me help you, Tom." Annie lifted his pack and Tom clipped his hip belt.

"Okay Tom?"

"Yeah, thanks." Tom clipped his chest strap and headed out.

The trail slowly worked its way up until the Cat Mountain junction. Then there seemed to be a slight downhill trend. Annie stopped at the shore of Cat Mountain Pond for a short break, a slug of water and a look up.

"That's where we were yesterday, Tom! Wow it sure looks like a long way up, doesn't it?"

"Well let me put it to you this way. I sure would hate to fall off. It's a straight down fall all the way to the pond."

They again headed down the trail. It wasn't long before they were at Cow horn Junction. Annie stopped, turned around and put her backpack against a tree.

"How are you doing, Tom?"

"I'm doing well, It's the uphill that gets me."

Annie smiled, "We'll get used to it or die trying."

"I hear that."

The trail moved across a ridge and then headed down a slight grade to a fork.

"This is where we leave the main trail Tom. Cow horn Pond is this way."

They approached the lean-to and again had it all to themselves.

"How about a drink and a couple cookies?"

"Yeah, that sounds good. First I need to check on Mother Nature."

On his way back, Tom picked up an armful of wood for the evening campfire.

"You are starting to really impress me, Tom. You must like this stuff!"

"Annie, this is a whole new world for me. I have never in my life ever been camping before. It is truly beautiful out here and I love it."

After their cookie break they decided to pitch their tent and sleep on the ground. They occupied the lean-to as a place to sit, eat and relax. Once the tent was up Tom continued to gather more wood. The evening campfire was one of Tom's favorite things to do. He gathered the wood, built and maintained the fire until they were ready to resign themselves to bed.

Annie fixed chicken teriyaki for dinner. After she took care of the dishes, Tom started the fire. It was a warm and beautiful night. Annie put a ground cloth by the fire and spread her sleeping bag on top of it. She then lay down on the sleeping bag, close to the fire.

"Join me, Tom?" And he did. They watched the flames dance and gazed at the stars. Annie soon fell asleep. Tom went to the tent and grabbed his sleeping bag, opened it up and covered Annie with it. He slid in beside her and held her all night.

In the morning Annie awoke with Tom snuggled tight with his arm around her.

"Good morning Annie," as she rolled to her back.

"Good morning. I'm sure glad it didn't rain last night."

"It was a beautiful night. I have never seen stars as bright as I saw them last night."

"That's because there are no street lights here to block your view of the sky Tom."

"Is that it? Whatever it is, it's not hard to like. Besides the stars, the fresh air, the morning mist on the lake, the loons, the list just goes on and on."

Annie made coffee and breakfast as Tom began the packing up process.

"What's for breakfast today, Annie?"

"Just scrambled eggs and coffee."

"That's good enough for me!" After Tom had the sleeping bags packed and the tent folded and put away he sat with Annie in the lean-to.

"What is our plan for today, Annie?"

"I think we'll go back the way we came, past Glasby Pond until we hit the High Falls Junction. We'll turn off there and head for the falls. The not-so-spectacular falls, but still a falls. You'll see what I mean. We should be there around four o'clock I think."

"Okay. Well, I'll soak the fire and we should be ready to go, right?"

"Right!"

"Here, let me give you a hand with your pack, Annie." Tom lifted her pack and Annie slipped in the straps and fastened her hip and shoulder straps together. She in turn did the same for Tom. One quick look around, then they headed back up the trail.

Back up on the ridge to Cow horn Junction, they turned right and headed for Cat Mountain Pond. Here they paused for a minute with their packs against a tree. They drank some water. "Do we have any cookies left Annie?"

"Sure. In my left side pouch. Grab me a couple too, please." Tom grabbed the cookies and reclosed Annie's side pouch.

When they finished their break, Tom took one more look at Cat Mountain and then headed up the trail.

It was a beautiful day, blue skies, those big white puffy clouds, and a gentle breeze blowing. They passed the junction to Cat Mountain and bore left in the direction of Glasby Pond. Annie was in the lead, the trail was narrow and at times large rocks needed to be walked through carefully. A sprained ankle in the wilderness is no fun. Moving on at a steady pace, Tom and Annie barely slowed down as they passed Glasby pond. They reached the junction for High Falls and turned left.

Annie grabbed her water bottle and turned to face Tom.

"Need a break, Tom?"

"Sure!" He unsnapped his bottle, twisted off the top and took a big gulp. "Man, that's good stuff. I have never drunk so much water! Or ever realized how good it tastes. I'm going to make a change in my life. From now on I'm going to get into better shape and start taking better care of my body by eating and drinking sensibly."

"Yeah, okay Tom! We'll see when we get back home just how sensible you are. You'll grab a beer and order a pizza."

"Nope! You're looking at a brand new Tom. From now on its water and wilderness for me. And a little Annie, of course."

Annie chuckled, snapped her water bottle on her waist, turned and headed for High Falls.

They wandered through a beautiful evergreen forest and through a small bog area. Here they passed a huge beaver dam.

"Wow! Look at that Annie!"

"Impressive, isn't it? Beavers are the builders in the wilderness, kind of like you in a way."

They arrived at a junction, High Falls to the left and the Primitive Corridor to the right.

"We'll head for the falls Tom, and hopefully find a place to camp for the night."

"Why do you say it like that, Annie?

"It's a popular spot, if I remember it right. A lot of the kids from the Ranger School take this loop. They stay here or at High Rock, another popular spot. I was only here once." The water rushing over the falls makes for a real good night's sleep."

"That will be another new experience in the wilderness for me Annie. How many more have you got up your sleeve?"

Annie just smiled. "The possibilities are endless Tom!"

Walking into High Falls, Annie noticed a canoe in front of the west lean-to.

"Someone is over there, probably came in to fish above the falls. I guess the trout fishing here is pretty good. The first camp site is empty. Let's wander on up to the east lean-to Tom, if it's empty we'll use that instead of pitching our tent." They wandered to the top of the falls, then turned left.

"Luck is on our side again Tom."

"Great, lets get out of these packs and look around."

Tom grabbed the water filter and their two water bottles and went to the river. Again he was caught up in the scene as he stood at the top of the falls, gazing downstream. He finally came back to reality and filled the two bottles.

When he wandered back to camp. "I thought I would have to come looking for you Tom. You've been gone awhile."

"I just can't get over just how beautiful it is. Everywhere we go, it's a new look, a new scene, like an artist's painting, absolutely beautiful. I just can't get over it. I had no idea this world even existed."

Annie just smiled. "You're already on my good side. You don't have to say anymore."

"I can't help it, it's true. I love it out here! But a couple of bonus points would be nice."

Annie still smiling. "Drink your water."

When they finished they changed out of their sweaty cloths. Annie opened up their sleeping bags and Tom started gathering some firewood for the evening fire.

"Man, the woods are almost picked clean Annie. It's hard to find any wood."

"I told you it was a popular spot. If you can't find any, we'll survive."

"No I'll find enough. It's just scarce." While Tom scoured the woods for firewood Annie fixed dinner and went to the river for more water.

Tom sat on the ground and leaned his back against the front of the lean-to. They dined on chili-mac and chocolate chip cookies. After dinner Annie made coffee and Tom started the fire. They sat together in front of the lean-to, watching the fire and talking endlessly of plans for the future.

Morning came and Tom rolled out of his sleeping bag to answer nature's call. When he returned to the lean-to, Annie was up and had the water boiling. She pulled on her boots, blew her hair out of her eyes and staggered into the woods yelling over her shoulder in a gruff voice, "COFFEE!!!"

Tom smiled, "I HEAR THAT!!" When Annie returned, her coffee was ready and more water was on the way.

"Wow, what time did we go to bed, Tom?"

"I don't know. We talked forever. I lost all track of time."

While they drank their first cup of eye opening coffee, company came walking up the trail.

"Hello in camp," a man said.

Annie replied, "Come on in. The coffee is hot."

"No thanks," he said as he came on in with his canoe on his back. "I'm just walking around the falls, headed upstream to do some fishing. I'll be back around noon time. And you folks?"

"We'll be gone by then. We're headed for High Rock today."

"Well, enjoy."

"You too." And the gentleman walked on through.

With her eyes now open, Annie fixed breakfast as Tom rolled up the sleeping bags and began the task of packing up. He filled the water bottles and grabbed a pot full for last night's fire, which was completely cold.

"Better to be safe, I guess."

"Your eggs are hot Tom, and your coffee is getting cold."

Tom sat down in the lean-to and joined Annie for breakfast. "How are you feeling, Annie?"

"Like I never slept. We must have talked all night."

"We may have. Like I said, I lost all track of time."

Tom packed away the pot. He took one more look around, then lifted Annie's backpack and helped her get hooked up. She did the same for Tom and again they hit the dusty trail.

"Any idea how far it is to High Rock, Annie?"

"We should be there by two."

"Oh, just a walk in the park, I guess."

"Yeah, it's all flat, too."

The trail was wide enough in places that Tom was able to walk beside Annie and talk the day away. They passed by more beaver dams and a few bog areas. This section of trail was an old railroad bed, used in the logging era.

Tom and Annie arrived at High Rock a little after two in the afternoon. The afternoon temperature had been warm.

As they walked into an empty campsite. "Let's put on our swimsuits and go for a swim Tom."

"That sounds like a plan to me."

It's not a deep hole but it's a refreshing one." And it felt really good as they just soaked in the water cooling their sweaty body's.

"Wow, that was just the ticket Annie."

They changed their clothes, pitched their tent and opened their sleeping bags. "Before we start gathering fire wood Annie, how about a couple cookies and a sit down with a drink. I'm a little dry." They sat with their backs against a tree.

"You know Tom, this is what I call a total unwind."

Annie handed Tom two cookies and took two for herself.

"There are just four left Tom."

"Well I don't think we should let them spoil, do you?"

"Yeah, let's finish them up. We'll be headed home tomorrow and we don't need to pack them out. Besides tomorrow the body is a temple, remember?"

Tom just looked at Annie and smiled. Annie looked at Tom. "Yeah, I thought so."

They finished their break and began the task of finding fire wood. Annie got things ready for dinner. With the work done Annie took Tom up onto High Rock. It was a perch overlooking the Oswegatchie River, a winding waterway twisting its way through the bog area below.

"It looks like a clear afternoon today. We'll come up here after dinner and watch the sun set. We are looking west right now Tom."

"Cool, we haven't seen the sun set since we've been out here."

"Well, unless you are on the top of a mountain it's hard to see the horizon when you're in the Adirondack Park."

They wandered back to the campsite and Annie started the water for dinner. It was the last of the freeze-dried food.

"We'll have light packs tomorrow walking out, Tom."

"Good. How far is it, do you know?"

"About four miles of really easy walking. We can be at the truck in two hours."

"And too soon Annie it will be over."

"Over? OVER? This is just the beginning, Tom. As soon as we get back we'll start planning the next trip. It's far from over."

They finished dinner, fixed a cup of coffee and made their way back up on High Rock. It was a sunset of all sunsets, taken right off the canvas of a landscape artist -- reds, oranges with dark streaks and white hues that words just cannot describe. Tom's arm wrapped around Annie and he held her tight all evening long. With a gentle kiss on her temple. "I do love you Annie."

"I love you too, Tom."

As the sun disappeared into the horizon, it marked the end of another wonderful day, a wonderful day in their lives together.

In the morning, Tom again rolled out and wandered into the woods to the latrine to answer nature's call. Returning to camp, he lit the stove and started heating the water for breakfast.

"Annie! it's a beautiful morning. Get up. Today I'll take you out to lunch if you get up."

"Make it room service Tom."

"Nope, that won't work." Tom opened the tent and grabbed her sleeping bag by the foot and dragged her out of the tent.

"What are you doing?"

"I'm taking you out to lunch. But first you need a bath!"

"NO, she screamed, NO.!"

"Yes, yes." And Tom pulled her sleeping bag off of her. He reached down and grabbed her by the arm, put her over his shoulder and headed for the river.

Annie laughed and screamed all the way there. "Please don't throw me in. I'll go in on my own."

Tom put her down and let her stand on the rock. Holding Tom's hand she grabbed his wrist, spun around and pushed him in. Completely surprised, Tom hit the water with a splash. He jumped to his feet, soaking wet.

With a look of total surprise. "Oh no, what just happened?"

Annie gave a little hop, turned, and with a laughing little scream ran back to the camp.

"You've been had, Tommy Blake."

"Yes I have, in a big way, for sure, but payback can be a bitch!" Annie continued to laugh. "You started it!"

Smiles covered their faces as they packed up their camp. Sleeping bags rolled up, tent put away and the fire soaked down. Tom helped Annie with her pack and Annie helped with Tom's. One quick look around and they hit the trail. The four mile walk was flat and easy. They signed the last register and headed for their truck. It was just noon.

"I'll stop at the store, Annie, and grab a water if you want."

"A water? Wow, I'm impressed. Maybe the body is a temple after all."

"I'm really kind of hungry Annie."

"There is a restaurant on the Oswegatchie River, just around the corner Tom."

"Let's get a bite to eat there before we head for home."

"Okay, sounds like a plan. I'm a little hungry myself Tom."

It was just a short hop to the restaurant. Tom and Annie both had a sandwich and a cold drink.

"That should hold me until we can hit Lillie's Diner Tom. We should be able to drive home, unpack, take showers and get to the diner just about dinner time."

"That works for me."

Tom drove the truck to the end of the Wanakena Road and turned left toward Star Lake. Within a mile Annie's eyes were closed. The drive to Adams Center was uneventful. When Tom pulled into the driveway, Annie opened her eyes.

"Why are we stopping, Tom?"

"Oh, I don't know, maybe because we're home."

"No way," Annie sat up. "Wow, I must have been tired. Or maybe I got too much fresh air. That tends to help a person get a good night's sleep."

Tom unloaded the truck and put everything in the kitchen to be washed before he put it away. Annie took a nice hot shower and washed her hair.

"Tom! The water is hot. I'll start a load of laundry while you take a shower. After you get dressed we can go to Lillie's for dinner."

"Okay. I can't wait to tell Lillie about our camping trip."

Tom opened the door to the diner and Annie walked in.

"Look whose back home," Lillie said with a smile when she turned to see who was walking in. "Well did you two have a good time?"

"I'll let Tom fill you in Lillie."

"Oh Lillie, there are not words to describe the wonderful, beautiful world that Annie introduced me to. Peaceful were the mornings, a light fog over the ponds, loons calling in the distance. The vista from a mountain top, the allure of a campfire under a vast canopy of stars, and beautiful forests of trees, rocks and rolling hills that seem to go on forever. And top that off with the most beautiful sunset I have ever seen. I have never been exposed to such a beautiful world as the one Annie just introduced me too. We have plans to become Forty-Sixers, to spend as much time as we can in the Adirondacks."

That was their first trip to the mountains, a most memorable trip that spawned the love affair of two young people and a journey through the Adirondack Mountains together.

# Late Afternoon
## Chapter Six

Tom realized he needed to get something to eat. He hadn't eaten since the reception. Cooking was completely out of the question. Lillie's was the answer. Tom walked out the front door and got into his truck. With the turn of the key it fired up and drew the attention of his neighbor Donna. She quickly ran to her kitchen window to see Tom backing out his driveway. As he drove to the main road, Donna saw the young woman sitting next to Tom.

"That's it. I know something is going on. Who is this woman? She acts like she's more than a relative, or even a friend. I think she's living there with him and Annie's funeral services were yesterday. I'm going to the police first thing tomorrow."

Tom drove to Lillie's Diner, parked his truck, and then walked into the diner. Lillie heard the door close, looked up and immediately walked over and gave Tom a heartfelt hug.

"Oh Tom, We're all so very sorry for your loss. Annie was a wonderful woman. What happened, do you know?"

"She was unconscious, lying on the floor, when I came home from work. I called 911 but in my heart I knew it was too late. The hospital performed an autopsy but all of the test results are not back yet. She was so active, and in excellent physical health. I just can't imagine what happened!" Tom continued, "When I know, you'll be on my list to call, okay?"

"Okay Tom. Again, you have our deepest sympathy."

Tom sat at a table for two on the back wall and ordered one of Annie's favorites, a BLT on wheat toast and a handful of chips. He sipped on a cup of black coffee. When he finished he went to the register to settle up with Lillie.

"That's okay, Tom. Just take care of yourself, okay?"

"Okay, thanks Lillie. I'll stay in touch."

Tom left the diner and drove back to the house. Donna heard the truck and ran to the kitchen window. Tom was just closing the front door when she managed a look in that direction. She wasn't sure if "she" was with him or not.

*"It's almost time for the news,"* Tom thought. He went to the living room and sat down in his chair, grabbed the remote and turned on the TV. His mind was clearly not on the news. He gazed off into space, with Annie on his mind and a smile on his face.

# Working Out

## Chapter Seven

After their trip to the Adirondacks, Tom started a routine to get himself into shape: arise early every morning, at 5:00 a.m., put on his sneakers, shorts and a T-shirt, open the front door and go. The first days were tough. It appeared he had no wind at all. As the days turned into weeks the distance grew. By the end of the summer he was running five miles every morning.

Annie was so impressed with Tom and his dedication that she would often join him. She was no slouch. Annie had no trouble keeping up with Tom and usually would sprint the last quarter mile home. Five times out of five, she beat him. Tom was steadily closing the gap, forcing Annie to tend to business. She knew it was only a matter of time until he caught her. But until he did she knew he would keep on training. Her strategy was working and working well.

September came and the school year was in full swing. Annie's smile was always present, in school, and at home. She loved the kids, her job and most of all Tom! Life was good.

Tom was busy on the job. He was involved in the construction of a senior citizen complex in Watertown. The contractor in charge offered the men overtime until the structure was closed in. Tom was more than happy to make some extra money.

When he returned home from work the first Friday after school started, Annie was waiting for him at the picnic table with an ice cold lemonade. Tom exited his truck and saw Annie waiting for him. As he walked in her direction he asked, "What's up?"

"I want to talk to you about something."

"Okay," he said. Tom sat down beside Annie and destroyed half of his lemonade. He placed the glass back on the table. "Oh that was good. Thanks Annie."

"I guess you were thirsty."

"A little, I think it's just that you make the best lemonade. You have me curious Annie, what's on your mind?"

Annie looked at Tom, "I think we're ready for our first high peak. I have Columbus Day off from school. That makes it a three day weekend. I think we can climb Cascade and Porter. They are close together and are rated as an easy climb. Columbus Day is in October. That's early enough that it won't be too cold and the colors may be at their peak. It should be beautiful in the park that time of year. I'm sure you won't be disappointed. What do you think Tom?"

"If you think we're ready let's do it! I've been ready since we got back from Wanakena. I can't wait to get started." Tom finished his lemonade, looked back at Annie with an ear to ear smile. "I love you Annie."

Annie threw her arms around Tom's neck holding him as if she would never let him go. "I love you, too, Tom."

# Morning, Day Two
## Chapter Eight

Tom was up at his usual 5:00 a.m. He put on his sneakers, shorts and a T-shirt and walked out the door. A few stretches, a quick look at the beautiful morning, and he was off. *"This is the type of morning Annie would join me on my run. But not today, I guess. Oh how I miss her."*

Donna was at her kitchen window again and she watched Tom exit the house and do his stretches and get ready for his run. And who was right beside him? *"That young woman. She had spent the night again."* Donna quickly called to Bob upstairs.

"Bob, Bob, come down here. You have to see this!"

Bob came running down the stairs and into the kitchen.

"Yeah? See what?"

"It's Tom and that woman. They're going running this morning. I'm telling you, something has been going on. You just don't get that friendly with another woman the day after your wife's funeral."

Bob walked to the window to look just in time to see Tom going around the corner.

"I saw Tom but I didn't see anyone else. Donna, give it a rest, will you?" Bob turned and walked back upstairs.

Donna left the kitchen window to fix Bob his breakfast. She sputtered to herself every minute Bob was gone. *"Tom did something to Annie, I just know it. He has his girl friend already moved in, that bastard! I'm going to the police this morning. I'll find out if they have any suspicions of their own. I'll tell them what I have seen. Maybe they will investigate."*

Bob came down stairs and sat at the table.

"Where are you off to today, honey?"

"I have to go to Albany today, Amsterdam tomorrow, and then I'll stop in Syracuse on my way home. I'll be home on Wednesday afternoon, unless I get caught up in a mess at one of the stores. Is there anything you need from me before I go?"

"Can't think of anything."

Bob finished his breakfast and took his coffee to go.

"Okay, see you Wednesday. Love you!"

"Love you too, Bob. Drive carefully."

Bob left the house, hopped in his car and drove away.

Donna picked up the table and loaded everything in the dish washer. She noticed Tom running toward the front porch, and right beside him was the young woman. Together they walked up the front steps and sat in the porch swing. The young woman held Tom's arm and laid her head on his shoulder. Tom just sat there with his head resting on the back of the swing as he seemed to catch his breath.

# A Surprised Annie
## Chapter Nine

As Tom rested on the front porch, a big smile came on his face as he remembered the day he had proposed to Annie. It was one of those lazy summer Sundays. Not enough time to go to the mountains, but you really wanted to do something. Tom grabbed their canoe and strapped it to the top of his truck. He threw the life jackets in the back, along with a couple of paddles. To the kitchen he went, found the loaf of bread, made a couple of chicken sandwiches and placed them in a small cooler. He also placed four bottles of water and two napkins, a bottle of wine and two wine glasses. Tom then went upstairs, where he had the diamond ring hidden away. He tucked it away in his jeans pocket and yelled to Annie.

"Yeah Tom?"

"I need one of those canvas grocery bags."

"They're down here in the kitchen silly. Why would they be upstairs? And what do you need one for?"

"I thought we would go for a swim and I could put a change of clothes and a couple of towels in it. So what do you say, good idea or not?"

"That sounds great to me. I'll change into a pair of cut off jeans, my sports bra and a T-shirt." Annie got changed and trotted downstairs and out the front door. Tom was all ready in the truck.

"Where are we going, Tom?"

"One of the guys at work told me about a place called Lakeview. Ever heard of it?"

"No can't say that I have."

"Well, it'll be a new adventure for both of us." They headed down Route 3 to Pierrepont Place. "He said it's down in here." Tom drove to the end of the road, to a small parking lot with a boat launch.

"I guess we put in here and paddle south until we hit the main stream. That will take us all the way to the lake."

"Okay," Annie with an excited smile. "Let's do it!"

Tom unloaded the canoe from the truck as Annie grabbed the paddles and life jackets. Tom went back to the truck for the cooler and canvas bag.

"That's it, that's everything Annie." He put everything in the canoe and shoved off with Annie in the bow.

Paddling south, they soon left the pond. They met a couple of fellows fishing and one other canoe.

"So far this is okay Tom. We almost have it all to ourselves."

They continued south until they hit the main stream. The current was slow but they were able to see which way was downstream. Tom and Annie soon came upon the outlet to the lake. There were a few more people here with big boats and small boats, kayaks and canoes.

"Well, I didn't expect to see this Annie. Let's go out into the lake and down the shore until we find a more private spot."

"Well, just how private do you need, Tom?"

"Just private enough so we can be alone."

"Depending on what you have on your mind, maybe we should have stayed home." Looking over her shoulder smiling.

"No, nothing like that."

They paddled down the shore a short distance until there was no one else around and then paddled on a little further.

"This looks good Annie." Tom turned the canoe and headed for shore. Annie jumped out grabbed the bow and gave it a yank. As Tom was getting out Annie stood with her hands on her hips looking at the vast emptiness. "Wow, this is cool! I don't know why I've never heard of this place! It's really nice. This beach seams to go on forever. Kind of like what you see in Hawaii, just miles of secluded beach."

Tom grabbed the cooler and the canvas bag and carried them away from the shore. "Come on, let's go."

Tom ran into the water with Annie close behind. Tom swam out until he could no longer touch bottom. Treading water, he waited for Annie. When she got close he dove down under her and came up behind her. Annie spun around as Tom threw his arms around her and gave her a great big kiss, a loving long passionate kiss that left them motionless. They sank to the bottom. Tom released her but Annie held on until she could no longer hold her breath. She then kicked for the surface. Annie gasped for air when she surfaced and Tom was right behind her. He again held her waist as she held his shoulders. They treaded water together and kissed again.

"I love you, Tommy Blake."

"Oh Annie, I could never love anyone but you."

They swam back to shore, grabbed their towels, dried off a bit and sat together on the beach. The sun felt really good as they just sat together and made idle chitchat.

In the late afternoon, Tom went to the cooler.

"I made us a couple of chicken sandwiches. Would you like one?"

"Sure, thank you Tom."

"I was starting to get a little hungry. I also brought some water. You know it's better for you than soda!"

Annie smiled. "Still working on that 'the body is a temple,' huh?"

Tom just chuckled.

Annie finished her sandwich and asked, "How long are we going to stay?"

"I'm thinking till sunset maybe, why?"

"I'm a little chilly in these wet clothes. I'll go over the sand dune and change."

While she was gone Tom got out the wine and glasses. He also put on dry clothes. There was no one else around so he changed on the beach.

When Annie returned, the wine and glasses were in the sand between their towels.

"Wow, what's this Tom, wine?"

"Yes! I was thinking we could have a glass of wine and watch the sun set. It's just you and me. Everyone else has left, so why not?"

Annie smiled, "That does sound nice. Okay, why not? I'm sure we can find our way back in the dark."

"Well, if we don't, we just sleep on the beach."

Tom poured the two glasses of wine and lifted his glass in toast.

"To us."

"To us," Annie repeated, and they each took a sip. Tom lay on his side and held his head with his hand. Annie sat against him as they watched the sun begin to set. Quietly, they sipped their wine and gazed at the western sky. It was a sunset to remember -- the calm water, gentle breeze, and a beautiful sunset.

*"This is perfect,"* Tom thought. He slowly reached in his pocket and gently pulled out the ring. "The sunset marks the

end of another beautiful day. Annie let's start a new day, a new life, as husband and wife. Will you marry me, Annie Marie Asland?"

Tom held the ring in front of her. Annie gasped for air, her eyes opened wide as she held her mouth with her left hand. She was unable to speak as she stared at the ring and Tom. Tears welled up in her eyes as she nodded yes. Tom placed the ring on her left hand as the tears rushed down her face. Annie bawled as she hugged Tom around his neck. Tom gently kissed her on the neck. "I love you Annie."

Barely able to compose herself and speak through her tears. Annie looked into Tom's eyes. "Oh I love you too Tom." Wiping the tears from her eyes. "Wow, you really know how to sweep a girl off her feet. I had no idea. This is beautiful. I love it. I love you," as she continued to sniffle and wipe her eyes. "Oh, I just don't know what to say. I'm stunned, I'm completely overwhelmed. How long have you been planning this?"

"For a while now, I wanted just the right moment."

"Oh Tom, the moment couldn't have been any more perfect. Thank you." Annie continued to smile uncontrollably with tears still in her eyes. She hugged Tom around the neck as tight as she could and refused to let him go. She was filled with emotion and the tears kept coming. Tom and Annie made love on the beach that night. Passionate, intimate love, like never before, their bodies entwined with each other.

They lay on the beach and held each other in silence for hours. Then Annie asked, "You planned this so well. Do you have a plan for the wedding?"

"As a matter of fact, I do. I picked the date and you can pick the place. Do you have a place in mind Annie?"

"Anywhere I want?"

"Anywhere."

"You said you have the date. How much time do I have?"

"Not much, just about a month."

"Wow, what would you have done if I said no?"

"I don't know. The thought hadn't crossed my mind."

"A month, huh?"

"Yes, I plan to have a small get together Friday night for a kind of a reception. Then be married Saturday morning and leave for our honeymoon right after the service, Columbus Day weekend."

"Oh Tom, that's a wonderful plan. Starting our life together and starting the High Peaks on our honeymoon. I couldn't have asked for anything more!"

The moon was full as it came up over the tree line. "We should head back Annie. It's getting late." They picked everything up, put it in the canoe and shoved off. The moon was so bright it wasn't hard to see their way back. The paddle was a little over an hour in the silence. The only noise was peepers and the croaking frogs. Neither Tom nor Annie spoke a word as they paddled. As the canoe slid up on shore at the boat launch, Annie jumped out grabbed the bow and pulled it in. When Tom climbed out, Annie said "I have it!"

"Have what?"

"A place to get married! You said that is my choice, right?"

"Right. Where do you have in mind?"

"Talcott Falls, just outside of Adams Center." Annie smiling from ear to ear. "What do you think?"

"I love it. That's perfect!"

# Police Investigation
## Chapter Ten

Donna watched out her kitchen window as Bob drove out of the driveway. She quickly headed upstairs to ready herself for work. Hair brushed, makeup on and dressed, she was work-appropriate. Walking through the kitchen, she was headed for her car. Donna paused by the telephone. *"Should I or shouldn't I?"* She opened the drawer which held the Greater Watertown Area Phonebook. Flipping through the white pages to New York State, subtitle POLICE. She pulled a pencil from the drawer and jotted down the number.

Pausing for just a moment of hesitation, she dialed the number.

"New York State Police, Sergeant Williams."

"Yes, my name is Donna Thompson. I wonder if I may speak to a homicide detective."

"Are you reporting a homicide?"

"No! I mean, I'm not sure. I think something funny is going on."

"Funny ma'am?"

"You know what I mean. Suspicious, maybe. Oh I don't know!" Donna hung up. She turned and headed for the door. Before she had taken two steps the phone rang. Donna turned around and answered the phone.

"Hello?"

"Yes, this is Sergeant Williams of the New York State Police. If you have a concern we would like to hear it."

"Oh, I don't know. My husband says to give it a rest."

"Give what a rest, ma'am?"

"It's my neighbor. His wife died and he has a young woman living with him already."

"When did she die?"

"Not even a week ago. I noticed her, this younger woman, at Annie's reception after the funeral."

"Well, could it be a daughter, or another relative, a sister, a niece that is staying there?"

"I'm not sure, they had no children, and I believe they were both only children. I just don't know who it could be!"

"Well, Mrs. Thompson, I'll pass this on to a detective. Do you have a number where he can reach you?"

"Yes, I'll give you my cell number." Donna recited the number to the desk sergeant.

"Okay, Mrs. Thompson, a detective will be calling you."

"Do you have any idea when?"

"I would suspect sometime this afternoon. Thank you for calling."

With that Donna hung up the phone. She then grabbed her chest to feel her heart pounding. *"I hope I'm not making a big mistake!"*

Donna left the kitchen and walked to her car. She opened the car door and slid into the front seat and glanced over to the porch where Tom was sitting. The young woman was still beside him. When Donna's car started Tom lifted his head and looked in her direction. He hesitantly raised his right hand in an effort to wave. Donna smiled and waved back then drove away.

Donna pulled into her usual spot at school, locked her car and entered the side door like a normal day. But normal was far from the way she felt. It was difficult to keep her mind on her work as she sat at her desk. She continued to think about Tom, the young woman and the things the sergeant said, over and over, picking out more details in her mind.

Finally it was her break time. Donna went to the teachers' lounge for a cup of coffee. Entering the lounge, she went straight to the coffee pot, grabbed her cup and paused to stare. There on the shelf right beside her cup was Annie's. "Teacher of the Year, Mrs. Annie Blake." Donna was instantly overcome with emotion. Her eyes began to tear up and she lost all control and began to cry. "Oh Annie, I miss you so." Another teacher, Emilie, jumped up and gave Donna a hug and patted her on the back.

"Oh Emilie, I feel like a fool."

"Not at all Donna. You and Annie were very close. It is to be expected."

Donna regained her composure, wiped her eyes and sat down. "Please forgive me, I don't know what came over me."

"Donna, don't worry about it. Just take a moment and drink your coffee. You'll get yourself together in a minute."

"Thank you, I think I'll take Annie's cup and give it to her husband Tom. I'm sure he would want it." With that Donna finished her coffee and took Annie's cup back to her office and placed it in her purse.

At three-thirty that afternoon, Donna's cell phone began to ring. Donna fumbled through her purse to find her phone. Quickly she answered it before it stopped ringing.

"Hello."

A stern voice on the other end. "Donna Thompson?"

"This is she."

"Donna, this is Detective Whallin of The New York State Police. Do you have a moment?"

"I'm at work!"

"When do you get off?"

"I'm done at 4:00 p.m."

"May I stop by and talk to you at 4:00?"

"Okay. I work at the Adams Center building of The South Jefferson School District."

"Can I meet you in the parking lot by your car?"

"Yes, that would be alright."

"I'll be driving an unmarked car. No one will know that I'm police."

"I'll be waiting by my car in the back row. It's a fairly new Chey, black with a New York dealer plate."

"I'll see you around four o'clock Mrs. Thompson."

At 4 o'clock, Donna shut down her computer, picked up her purse, then walked out of her office. The hallway was quiet since almost everyone had left the building. As she walked to her car, she was looking for the detective's car. She wasn't sure what to look for. When Donna reached her car she stood by the door, fumbling through her purse, pretending to look for her keys. A dark blue sedan pulled up beside her.

"Looking for something ma'am?"

"No, for some*one* actually. Are you Detective Whallin?"

"Yes. You must be Donna Thompson!"

"Yes, I am."

"Would you like to get in my car ma'am?"

Donna walked around his car and sat in the passenger's seat.

"Mrs. Thompson, please tell me your concerns about Annie Blake's death."

"Well, at the reception after her funeral, I saw a young woman holding Tom's arm, then she stood on her tip toes and gave him a kiss. The next day she stood on his porch drinking coffee, watching him weed Annie's garden. And then this morning they went running together. When they returned they sat in the swing on his front porch together. All of this is too soon after her death for me to swallow, if you get my gist detective."

"Well, Mrs. Thompson, does anyone else share your concerns?"

"My husband told me to 'give it a rest.' Those were his words!"

"Your husband has seen this also?"

"Well, no. Every time I try to point her out, she is gone, or he's not quick enough."

"So actually, you're the only one to see her?"

"Why, yes, I guess I am! But detective, I'm not imagining it. She is there. I've seen her with my own eyes!"

The detective reassured Donna, "I'm sure you have. And you're sure that she isn't a relative in town for the funeral?"

"No, I'm not sure of that. But I am sure that they had no children and that neither of them had any sisters."

"Well, Mrs. Thompson, after your call this morning I made a few calls myself. I called the coroner and asked if anything jumped out at him during the autopsy. He, the medical examiner, said that Mrs. Blake died around noon from a massive heart attack. In his words, she was dead before she hit the floor. The tox screen showed no evidence of any drugs in her system that would have caused her heart attack."

Donna listened intently.

"Mrs. Thompson, this is what I'm going to do. I'm going to pay Mr. Blake a visit. I'll tell him it is strictly routine, that after a mysterious death occurs we have to make an inquiry. I can usually tell if someone is trying to hide something."

"Thank you, Detective. My husband is probably right. I'm just imagining all of this. And I'm sending you on a wild goose chase. Thank you again, Detective."

"That is no problem, Mrs. Thompson."

Donna left the detective's car and got into her own, then made the short drive home. Upon entering her driveway, she saw Tom, just sitting on his front porch alone. Donna reached over the center console to grabbed her purse and saw Annie's coffee cup. She turned her head and looked at Tom again. *"There's no better time than the present."* Donna climbed out of her car and walked over to Tom's house.

"Hi, Tom. How are you doing?"

"Hi, Donna. Oh, I'm okay, I guess. I feel like I should go back to work but I really just don't feel much like it, you know?"

"I don't know Tom, but I can imagine your pain."

Tom got up and walked to the steps and sat in front of Donna.

"I miss Annie too Tom, so I can only imagine your pain, which brings me to the reason I came over."

Donna reached into her purse and pulled out Annie's coffee cup. "I saw this today and I knew you would want it."

With the cup in her hand, she reached out to give it to Tom. He gently took it from Donna, looked at it with a tear in his eye and read "Teacher of The Year, Mrs. Annie Blake." Then he choked, and desperately tried to control his emotions, to no avail. Tom turned, used his sleeve to wipe his tears, and then apologized to Donna.

"Please excuse me Donna."

"Oh, Tom, no. I'm the one who should apologize. I didn't mean to upset you."

"I'm sure you didn't."

Donna wanted to ask Tom about the young woman she had seen around the house, but she didn't want to upset him anymore. But in her mind she just had to know!

"Tom, remember I asked you about the young woman at the reception for Annie, the one that gave you the kiss? She acted like she was a real close friend of yours. Who is she, do you remember?"

"No, Donna, I really don't remember any kiss. The whole day is a blur. As far as a close friend of mine there is, and always has been, just one. That's Annie, and you know," Tom hesitated, tipped his head and said. "Even though she's gone I always feel her presence."

Donna slumped all the way to her toes. *"Bob was right. I'm a fool for calling the police. Why didn't I just mind my own business?"*

Donna placed her hand on Tom's. "Well, I'd better get home. I've upset you enough for one day. Again, Tom, I'm sorry."

"It's not your fault, Donna. It's just that I'm still emotional."

Donna turned to walk away.

"And Donna?"

She turned back toward Tom. "Yes?"

"Here, you take Annie's coffee cup. It's the one she kept at school, right?"

"Yes it is."

"Well, you were more a part of that side of her life than I was. I'm sure she would want you to have it. Keep it and never forget what a wonderful teacher she really was."

"Thank you, Tom. I won't ever forget."

Donna walked across the lawn to her house with her head hung low, more confused than ever. *"Tom is truly heartbroken over Annie's passing, but who is that young woman? He doesn't acknowledge her existence, but I know what I see! I see it almost every day and they are so open about it, sitting on the porch together, going for a run, and even drinking a cup of coffee on the porch together. Maybe I'm just losing my mind."*

Tom sat on the front steps for a while, just leaning against the post and gazing into space. Hunger finally set in, for the first time since the funeral. He stood up and walked to his truck. He backed from his driveway, then headed for Lillie's Diner. It was a short drive, only about a mile. It was only about 4:30, early for the dinner crowd, so Tom didn't have to mingle with anyone. Lillie heard the door slam, and turned to see Tom walking in.

"Hi, Tom," as she walked to his table. "How's it going?"

"It's okay, Lillie, day by day, you know."

"Well, you hang in there. It'll get better, you'll see."

"I'm sure it will, but it's really hard, you know?"

"I'm sure it is. Well, what can I get you?"

"What's the special?"

"Meatloaf, mashed potatoes and carrots."

"Yeah, that sounds good, with a glass of water please."

"You've got it Tom." Lillie walked to the back counter and yelled, "ORDER!" Grabbed him a bottle of water, a clean glass, a napkin and silverware and returned to Tom's table.

"Have you gone back to work, Tom?"

"No, not yet, Lillie. I just don't have any drive, you know. But today is the first day I have an appetite, so I don't think it will be much longer. I'll get my ass moving again."

Lillie placed her hand on Tom's shoulder. "It would probably be the best thing for you. It would take your mind off things, if you know what I mean."

"Yes, I know Lillie, you're probably right."

"ORDER UP!" Came from the back and Lillie turned walked to the back and grabbed Tom's dinner. She also picked up a bottle of ketchup, then returned to Tom's table.

"Enjoy Tom." Then left him to eat in peace.

Tom finished his dinner and Lillie yelled to him across the empty diner, "Fresh apple pie today, Tom."

"Thanks, Lillie, but I can't. I'm stuffed. What do I owe you?"

"Six dollars."

Tom placed a five and two ones on the table. "Very good, Lillie. Thanks."

"You're welcome, Tom, It's always good to see you."

Tom walked out and returned to his truck. After a short drive back home, Tom noticed a strange car in front of his house. He pulled his truck into its usual spot, put it in park and shut off the engine. As he slid from the driver's seat, a man got out of the car and walked toward Tom's truck.

"Thomas W. Blake?" asked the man, dressed in a pair of tight jeans, western shirt, a string tie and a wide brimmed hat. Tom also noticed a badge on his belt under his denim jacket.

"Yes, I'm Thomas Blake. Can I help you?"

"I'm Detective Whallin of the New York State police. Do you have a few minutes so we could talk?"

"Sure, but can we go somewhere comfortable? We don't need to stand out here, do we?"

"No, anywhere is fine with me."

"Have you had your afternoon coffee, Detective?"

"A coffee would be fine." Detective Whallin was instantly suspicious as he thought, *"He doesn't want me here! Where does he want to go?"*

"Where do you have in mind, Mr. Blake?"

"Well, my kitchen, if you don't mind the mess. I haven't been the best housekeeper since my wife died."

"It's fine, I'm sure, Mr. Blake." Detective Whallin was totally taken aback. He wasn't expecting to go inside. *"This will give me a chance to look around."* ·

Tom walked up the front steps, reached in his pocket for his keys and unlocked the door. *"Strange, why would you lock the door if another woman is here?"*

Tom entered the house, with the detective close behind. They entered the living room and walked toward the kitchen. The detective noticed a throw pillow on the floor, next to what appeared to be a man's chair with a blanket thrown carelessly on it. *"Looks like he sleeps there."*

Speaking in a sad voice. "It will only take a minute Detective. How do you drink your coffee?"

"Black, Mr. Blake."

"Pull yourself out a stool and make yourself comfortable, Detective."

Tom had the coffee perking in just a minute and pulled out a couple of cups from the cupboard. "I'm sorry I don't have any cookies to munch on."

"Do you live here alone, Mr. Blake?"

"Yes, sir. I was married, but my wife died last week."

"Yes, I know. That's why I'm here. It's standard procedure to investigate a death when someone dies for no apparent reason, as your wife did. She was really still a young woman. Did you notice any change in her demeanor? Was she feeling ill at all?"

"No sir, she was fine, except for the day she died. She was pale that morning and didn't feel well. I told her to stay home and get some rest. Annie agreed and called in sick to school."

The coffee was finished perking so Tom turned, grabbed the pot, and turned back to pour the detective a cup. Before putting it back, he also poured one for himself.

"Well, Mr. Blake, do you know what your wife died of?"

"I'm not sure. The doctor thinks she had a heart attack. But we haven't gotten the coroner's report yet, so I guess the answer is no, I really don't know for sure."

"When was the last time you saw your wife?"

"That morning, when I left for work."

"Did you talk to her at all that day?"

"Yes, I called her just before I broke for lunch. I asked her how she was feeling. Annie told me that she felt weak and tired. I asked her if she wanted me to take her to the doctor. She told me no, she just wanted to rest but if she didn't feel any better tomorrow we would talk about it."

"Was she on any medication that you know of?"

"No medication that I know of, anyway. We both take vitamins, but I haven't been feeling sick at all."

"Well, Mr. Blake, is there a history of heart problems in her family?"

"Why, yes, now that you mention it. Both of Annie's parents died of heart problems. I never put the two together before. But Annie was the picture of health. We jogged together, climbed mountains together and on weekends went for long walks together. She never gave me any indication that she wasn't feeling 100%."

Tom got up and grabbed the coffee pot and topped off their cups.

Whallin took another sip of his coffee. "Just a couple more questions Mr. Blake. Does your wife have any life insurance?"

"Life insurance? I'm not sure if you would call it that."

"What do you mean, Mr. Blake?"

"When we purchased our home, we were required to buy mortgage insurance. If one of us died, the mortgage would be paid. I'm not sure if you would call that life insurance. Other than that no, we do not have any other life insurance."

"My last question, Mr. Blake. Did your wife have a will?"

"A will? No, not a will per se. We both have living trusts. We had no children, and neither of us has any brothers or sisters. Annie's parents are gone, along with my dad. My mom lives in a nursing home in Georgia. The living trust gives everything to the surviving spouse. In the event that we died simultaneously, the estate would be sold. After executor's fees were paid, the remainder would be given to The Adirondack Mountain Club in our names."

"Well, Mr. Blake, I have Annie's autopsy report with me."

"Can you tell me what it says Detective?"

"Yes, I can. Annie died of a massive heart attack. There were no drugs found in her system. Not just any drugs that would cause a heart attack, but no drugs in her system at all. Also, there was nothing anyone could have done to save her. According to the coroner, she was gone before she hit the floor.

Tears began to fill Tom's eyes, and he turned his head away. "My deepest condolences Mr. Blake."

Tom choked back the tears, "Thank you."

"Well, I have completed my business here. Thank you for the coffee, Mr. Blake. I will complete my report on this matter. I'm sure that you won't be hearing from anyone else about this. Again, you have my deepest sympathy for your loss." Choking back emotion, Tom just nodded his head.

"I'll show myself out." Detective Whallin pushed in his stool, turned, walked through the living room and closed the front door behind himself.

The detective went to his car, opened the door and slid in behind the wheel. After starting the engine, he pulled away from the yard. At the end of the street he turned right and headed toward Watertown and his office. Detective Whallin entered his office and laid his briefcase on his desk and sat in his chair. He sat for just a minute, then pushed the intercom button and said, "Sergeant Williams?"

"Yes, detective."

"Any calls for me? I'm expecting a call from Donna Thompson."

"No, sir, your message board is empty."

"Okay, thanks."

The detective picked up his phone and dialed her number. The phone rang three times before Donna answered.

"Hello, Mrs. Thompson?"

"Yes, this is Donna Thompson."

"Detective Whallin here."

"Yes, Detective."

"I wanted you to know I spoke with Mr. Blake this afternoon. I found him to be very forthcoming and open to any questions that I had. He didn't appear to have anything to hide and I found no indication that there was anyone else living at his residence. With no hesitation he invited me in and we spoke over coffee. I observed that he is truly upset over his wife's death. It is very evident that the emotion has taken its toll on him. I am convinced he had absolutely nothing to do with his wife's death. In conclusion, I am closing this investigation. I hope this gives you some peace over your friend's untimely death."

"Yes, yes, Detective. You have made me feel much better. You have lifted an awful burden from my heart. Thank you so much."

"Thank you for your call Mrs. Thompson. And please don't hesitate to call if you have any more concerns. Good- bye."

"Good-bye, Detective, and again, thank you."

Donna hung up the phone and said to herself, *"Bob was right, so right. I must be delirious. Tom has always been nothing more than a loving husband. I should just mind my own business."*

# The Wedding

## Chapter Eleven

Tom dried the tears from his eyes and got hold of himself. He picked up the kitchen and rinsed the two cups. Tom emptied the coffee pot and put away the coffee. As he walked into the living room the house felt so empty that he became uneasy and had to leave. *"I need to be close to Annie right now. Where can I go?"* Tom got in his truck and drove to Talcott Falls. Parking his truck on the side of the road, Tom then walked down the bank to the stream's bottom and sat. Soon it all came back.

It was Friday afternoon. John and Marie Asland drove in from Georgia. We put them up at the Carriage House in Watertown. We just didn't have any room in the one-bedroom house we were renting. My parents, William -- Bill, as Annie always called him -- and mom, Rosemary to everyone else, arrived around six o'clock. They also had a room at the Carriage House. Annie and I arranged to meet them in the Carriage House Restaurant at seven for dinner and a few drinks. It was the first time our parents had met. It was a wonderful evening and everyone got along. We laughed, told stories of childhood mischief and those proud moments every parent loves to tell. Annie was aglow all evening.

Mrs. Asland asked what our plans were for a honeymoon. Annie grabbed my arm and held me close.

"Tom and I are going to climb Cascade and Porter Mountains in the Adirondack Park. They are the first two mountains in our quest to become Forty-Sixers."

"What are Forty-Sixers?" she asked.

I responded, "There are 46 high peaks over four thousand feet in the Adirondack Mountains. If you climb all 46 you become what is known as a Forty-Sixer. Annie and I WILL become Forty-Sixers."

Annie looked at me with a big smile and pulled me close for a kiss. Then Annie said, "I know it's not your traditional honeymoon, but it's truly what we want to do. We plan on leaving right after our wedding."

Rosemary said, "Speaking of wedding, we haven't heard your plans for it. Please tell us what we can expect, or are you keeping it a secret?"

"No secret," Annie said, "It's going to be very small. In fact, there will be only seven people there. We six and the justice of the peace."

Dad said, "Wow that is small. Where is it happening? Not on the top of a four thousand foot mountain, I hope!"

"Not quite," I said. "We have a spot picked out. A place called Talcott Falls. It's just outside Adams Center, right next to the road. No real hiking needed."

"Sounds like just what you two ordered," John said. "And who is standing up with you?"

"We thought that my parents would stand up with me and Tom's parents would stand up with him, if you will."

John and Marie said, "We would be happy to." Mom and dad said, "It will be our pleasure." Then Rosemary said, "Oh Annie, it all sounds so wonderful," as tears began to fill her eyes.

"May I propose a toast?" asked John. He raised his glass and we all followed. "To the two most wonderful kids we know. May you always be as happy as you are right now."

"Hear, hear!" and we sipped our wine. Annie was so happy. She had a glow I'll never, ever forget.

The party broke up just after eleven o'clock. Annie took her dress for the wedding and stayed with her parents at the hotel and I went back to our house for the night. There was that old wives' tale that I wasn't to see her after midnight on the day of the wedding. I didn't want to start out with any kind of bad luck. All I wanted was to be happy and healthy for the rest of my life with Annie!

Saturday morning came and I had a couple of hours to kill before the wedding. I threw on a pair of jeans and a shirt and drove to Lillie's for some breakfast. When I walked through the door, Lillie said, "Good morning, Tom. Where is Annie?"

"She stayed the night with her parents in Watertown."

"Oh, is everything alright?"

"Yeah, we weren't supposed to see each other after midnight."

"Oh, Oh, Oh! Are you two getting married today?" Lillie was almost jumping up and down, she was so excited. "Congratulations! Oh, Tom, I'm so happy for you two. Oh, I have a million questions. Are you going away? Where are you getting married? Oh, oh, never mind. I'll shut up. You can tell me all about it later. What can I get you for breakfast? It's on the house! Oh, I'm so excited!" Lillie grabbed my face and gave me a great big kiss on the cheek.

"Oh, Lillie, thank you. I'll have the special and a coffee."

"Coming right up. ORDER!"

When I left the diner, Lillie yelled to me "GOOD LUCK, TOM!" I responded with, "THANK YOU LILLIE." I drove home, took a shower, shaved and got myself ready. That's when I started to get nervous, nervous as hell! My stomach went bottom side up. I've heard of the jitters, but I never thought I'd get 'em. But I got 'em, I got 'em good!

I drove to the falls. The town justice was already there. Together we walked down to the base of the falls. We were only there a short while when Dad and Mom arrived. I was so happy when dad took mom's hand and helped her down the hill and stood beside me. When mom approached me she gave me a big hug and a kiss on my cheek. Dad smiled and wished me luck. "Remember son, we love you."

"Thanks, Dad. I love you guys, too."

John and Marie drove up in a rented car. John escorted Marie down the hill to the base of the falls where the rest of us waited. He returned to the car, opened the door and the most beautiful girl I have ever seen stepped out. My heart was ready to explode! My dad put his hand on my shoulder and said, "She's beautiful, son." With tears in my eyes, I could only nod. I was filled with emotion! So much I could only cry, and cry I did.

Annie took John by the arm and together they walked to the base of the falls. Marie took her place to Annie's left with John on her right. The town justice, Don, smiled, looked right at Annie and said, "Ready?" Annie nodded her head yes.

"We are gathered here in this beautiful place created by God, to join this beautiful couple in holy matrimony. If any-one knows why this couple should not be joined, let him speak now or forever hold his peace. Who gives this bride to be married?"

John and Marie said in unison, "We do!" Then Annie handed her flowers to her mother. John offered Annie's hand to me. With tears in my eyes, I could hardly see. I accepted her hand and she stepped forward. John took his place beside Marie, holding her hand.

I was so choked with emotion I could hardly repeat my vows, as the tears continued to well up in my eyes. Annie was barely able to speak. With the falls gently running behind us, the clouds opened up with a beautiful array of sunshine. Don pronounced us husband and wife, wife and husband.

"What God has joined together, let no man put asunder. You may kiss your bride, Tom!" I threw my arms around her, gave her a quick kiss and, choked with emotion, said, "I love you, Annie."

"Oh Tom," Annie, hardly able to speak, said, "I love you too."

Dad and mom gave Annie a hug and I shook John's hand and gave Marie a big hug.

"You take care of her. She's our only daughter."

I replied, "I'll do my best, I promise." I turned to Don, gave him twenty dollars and said, "Thank you."

"You're welcome and good luck."

I took Annie by the hand and helped her to the top of the bank. We turned around and waved good-bye. I said, "Thank you all for coming." Annie added, "We love you."

Our parents yelled, "GOOK LUCK, WE LOVE YOU TOO."

I opened the door for Annie and helped her in. I got behind the wheel, started the truck and blew the horn as we drove away.

We drove back home and tried to change our clothes but we were so filled with love and emotion that I couldn't keep my hands off her. We made love, took a shower and made love again. It was the most beautiful time of my life. And it only got better.

Sitting on the bank at the falls, remembering back, Tom's eyes were filled with tears. *"Oh Annie, I love you so. Please come back to me, please."* Tom continued to cry.

# A New House

## Chapter Twelve

Tom remained on the bank of the falls until he regained his composure. Thirty minutes passed before he stood, turned and walked to his truck. He desperately wanted something to drink, soda, water, lemonade, something, but knew Lillie's was no place to be in his current state of mind. *"I'll just get something at home,"* and drove on by Lillie's.

Tom parked his truck in the driveway, turned off the ignition and slid from the seat. He entered the house and went on into the kitchen, where he searched the refrigerator and found a ice cold soda. After downing about half the bottle Tom went to the sink and freshened his face with cold water. *"Wow that will throw anyone into shock!"* Tom opened the cupboard and noticed a box of mini muffins. *"Where were these when the detective stopped in. I'll take these and my soda to the porch."*

Tom sat down in the swing and began munching on the bag of muffins.

*"This porch is what sold Annie on this house, the flowers on the railing, flower gardens in front and facing the west to watch the sun sets. Oh, how she loved to watch the sun set. So many evenings we sat together here on this swing, sometimes never saying a word, just sitting together and watching the sun slowly disappear over the*

horizon. *Sometimes with all its glory and other times no glory at all, just the end of another day here, together."*

We were married only about five months when I noticed a "For Sale" sign on my way home from work. That's what we need, a house of our own, a garden for Annie and a garage with a shop for me. It's the all American dream, to own your own home.

At home, I quietly crept up behind Annie in the kitchen of the one-bedroom house we were renting, and put my arms around her waist and kissed her neck. "What's for dinner?" I asked.

"Wouldn't you like to know."

"I know that whatever you cook will be great. I had a flash on my way home today."

"Okay, what kind of flash? Light bulbs going off in your eyes, I-have-an-idea kind of flash, or a naked girl running in front of your truck kind of flash?"

I laughed and said, "I-have-an-idea kind of flash. Want to hear it?"

"You keep talking while I keep working on dinner. And I also have a flash. You can set the table while you're talking. What do you think of that flash?"

"I saw a 'For Sale' sign on a house on my way home today. I'm thinking maybe we should be looking for a house of our own. I really don't think we're going anywhere. You love your job, and I'm making good money at mine, and I like my boss. I think he treats me well. I don't think I'll do any better working for someone else. So if we're staying here, we should put our rent money into our own house instead of someone else's. Together with all the reasons I just mentioned, we are close to the Adirondack Mountains here. If we move away who knows how far away from them we'll be. So I'm thinking we should buy a house here and put some roots down."

There was a long pause. Annie said nothing. Tom finally said, "Well, what do you think?"

"I think you should pour the milk."

"Pour the milk?"

"Yes, pour the milk so we can eat our dinner! The quicker you pour the milk, the quicker we can eat and the quicker we can start looking at houses." Annie jumped into Tom's arms, threw her arms around his neck and started kissing him all over. "Oh, you wonderful man! I love you. I think it's a wonderful idea. I can't wait to start looking. Oh Tom, I'm so excited. You always say the right things." Annie continued kissing him all over. "I love you, I love you, I love you!"

Annie always had a way of making me smile. This day was no different. I was smiling from ear to ear.

Annie opened the oven and pulled out a pan of stuffed peppers and placed two on my plate and one on hers. "Wow, that looks good Annie. How about a slice of Italian bread?"

"Sure," she grabbed the bread, butter and a butter knife and sat down.

"How? What? Do you have any idea how we go about this Tom?"

"No, not really. I've never bought a house before. Maybe just go for a drive and look for houses with a "For Sale" sign in front."

"Sure, that sounds like a place to start. Let's go for a ride after dinner!"

"Sounds like a plan to me."

We finished dinner and rinsed off all the dishes, put the milk, butter and bread away and walked out the door. Annie started running toward the truck. "I'll race you!" She giggled and laughed as she skipped and ran to the truck and I laughed as I chased her. I never have been able to catch her. I get close but always come up a little short.

We first drove by the house I saw on the way home. "I'm really not interested in this house. It's just where I got the idea."

"Yes, I hear what you're saying. I really don't like it either."

We drove around for awhile but found only a couple of "For Sale" signs.

"How about this weekend Annie we call a couple of realtors? Maybe they can steer us to a few houses that are for sale."

"Yeah, that sounds like a good idea Tom."

We drove around for a little longer until it started to get dark. Then we headed for home. We were both so excited we lay in bed and talked about our new dream for hours. We discussed what we were looking for in a house. Annie wanted a big kitchen with a breakfast bar, a dining room, laundry room, so she didn't have to go to the Laundromat any more. We wanted three bedrooms: a master bedroom with an attached bath and two smaller bedrooms, one for a boy and one for a girl, if we were so blessed. And it had to have a porch, facing the west, so we could watch the sun set together.

"What are you looking for, Tom?"

"I don't need much. I'd like a garage, big enough so I could have a work shop, a back yard big enough that we can have a grill on a patio for an occasional cookout when our parents come to visit and a swing for that little boy and girl you're talking about."

Tom and Annie drifted off to sleep in each other's arms, dreaming of what the future might hold. Life was good.

Saturday morning found Tom and Annie at Lillie's diner for breakfast. They entered the diner. Lillie greeted them with a warm "Good morning, you two. What has you up so early on a Saturday morning?"

"Tom and I are looking at houses today. We've decided this is where we want to live, work and raise a family."

"Oh how wonderful. Raise a family? Are you pregnant?"

"No, not yet, but someday. There's no hurry."

"Buying your first house, that's so exciting! What can I get you for breakfast?"

"Two specials and coffee," Tom replied.

"Two specials coming up. ORDER!"

Annie had a telephone book in the truck and after break-fast they headed to Watertown to Sunrise Reality. They were greeted warmly by the owner of the business, Bill Baker.

"Good morning folks. Is there something we can help you with this morning?"

"We are looking for houses somewhere in the Adams Center area," Annie said.

"Okay. Why don't we start with coffee?" Bill asked. "Come on into the kitchen." They walked into a separate room with a starter kitchen. The coffee pot was ready and cups were on the table.

"Have a seat, folks. Do you take cream or sugar in your coffee?"

"Thank you, no. Just black," Annie responded.

Bill poured our coffee and one for himself. He grabbed a folder and handed it to Annie. "These are listings in a five mile radius around Adams Center. May I ask what you are looking for in a house?"

"Three bedroom, two baths, a front porch, a garage and a big back yard," Annie said. "Off the top of your head, do you have anything that would fill that bill?"

"Not exactly. I have a lot of two-bedroom, one-bath homes. Some are rural settings, in the country. I have a big old farm house, with no limitations on the size of the back yard," Bill chuckled.

We looked through all of Bill's listings and didn't see anything that interested us. We finished our coffee and thanked Bill for his time, but he didn't have anything for us at that time.

"Let me have your names and number and if anything comes in I think you would be interested in, I'll give you a call."

"That sounds good. Thank you very much," Tom said. Bill took our names and phone number and we returned to our truck.

"Who's next on the list Annie?"

"Let's go to North Country Homes on Washington Street Tom."

"That should be easy to find." It was, but they didn't have anything we were looking for either. Then we went on to Century Twenty-two, but again no luck. The story was the same everywhere we went. They just didn't have what we were looking for.

"Well, there is a small realtor in Adams, Pop's Realty on East Church Street Tom."

We drove on into Adams and found Pop's office in his residence. Pop greeted us at the door with a big smile. His walk was slow as he shuffled his feet and he never really stood up straight. He led us into his office and offered us chairs. "Are we looking for a house?" Annie said, "Yes." Pop smiled a big smile and said, "I thought so. A handsome young couple like yourselves, what else would you be looking for?"

Annie returned his smile and said, "Preferably a three-bedroom, two-bath in the Adams Center area. Is anything like that available?"

"No, not exactly like that. Not anything that I have listed anyway. Have you been to Watertown?"

"Yes we have. No luck there either."

"Well here's an idea for you. Build the house you want in the area you want to build it in."

Annie looked at me and I looked at her. "That's not a bad idea! Tom works for a contractor. Why didn't we think of that?" We stood up and thanked Pop for his time. Annie again had a big smile on her face.

Annie held Tom's arm all the way to the truck and asked, "What do you think Tom? Do you know how much work you have lined up?"

"I'm not sure. I know we're busy, but just how busy is the question."

They drove home and upon entering the house Tom went straight for the phone and dialed his boss, David's number.

"David Willard, can I help you?" the voice on the other end said.

"David, its Tommy Blake. How are you?"

"Good, Tom. What's up?"

Annie and I would like to have a house built this summer. Is there any chance that we could get it done?"

"Yeah, it could get done. Do you have the property?"

"No, we just got the idea this morning."

"Well, Tom, if you want to build this year you'll have to get in gear. First you have to find a lot. Closing on that alone takes about forty-five days. You'll need to make sure you have water, and get your plans approved and all the permits issued. I'm not trying to discourage you Tom, but I like to put things in motion at least a year before we break ground."

"Okay, thanks David. I'll let you know what we decide."

"Good-bye, Tom."

Tom hung up the phone, with Annie looking straight at him. "I can tell by the look on your face Tom, it's not going to happen, is it?"

"David say's he puts things in motion at least a year in advance. That doesn't mean we can't build our own home. It just means we can't build it this year. I'm sorry, Annie. The option is still there, just not quite what we had in mind."

"Well Tom, we'll keep looking, for a house already built, or for a piece of land we just can't live without." I liked her enthusiasm. One way or another we were going to have our own home!

We started getting the daily newspaper, checking the homes for sale every day. If something caught our eye we'd drive by and check it out. If it passed the drive-by look, our next step was to make an appointment for a walk-through. Nothing quite fit the bill. I never lost sight of our dream house and Annie maintained her enthusiasm. "It's out there, Tom. I know it is. We just haven't found it yet."

Annie went to the teachers' lounge one morning for her coffee and a short chit-chat with the girls. Donna Thompson asked, "Are you still looking for a house Annie?"

"Why yes, we are, why do you ask?"

"Well, my neighbor is going to put her house on the market. What are you looking for?"

"We would like a three-bedroom, two-bath with a big kitchen and a breakfast bar, a laundry room and a formal dining room. And most of all, a front porch facing the west, behind a flower garden for me. We'd like a garage big enough so Tom can have a workshop and a big back yard -- big enough for a patio with a grill and a swing set."

"A swing set? Annie, are you pregnant?"

"No, but maybe someday, God willing. Donna, can you tell me a little bit about your neighbor's house?"

"Yes, a little I can. I know it has three bedroom, two baths and the west facing porch with a garage. That's about all I'm sure of. Oh and the back yard is beautiful."

"It doesn't sound bad. Where is it?"

"It's right next to my house, on Horner Drive, just past the cemetery on your way to Adams."

"Okay, do you know the number?"

"We are 21, so I assume they are 19."

"Thanks Donna. I'll drive by on my way home tonight."

After school, Annie got into her car and as usual she drove on home, completely forgetting to go the other way toward Adams. Before exiting her car, she backed out of the driveway and did an about-face. *"Horner Drive is very close to school, 15, 17, 19 .... That must be the one. Oh how nice! Beautiful front porch, like Donna said, and it is facing the west. I can definitely do better with the flower gardens! The garage is attached, and it is a big one. Should I stop, or should I wait for Tom?"*

Annie decided to wait for Tom and began to drive on through. Donna stuck her head out her front door and waved to Annie to come in. Annie stopped her car in front of Donna's house and rolled down her window.

"Annie, come in!" Annie exited her car and walked to Donna. "What do you think?"

"I like what I see so far. Do you have a phone number for them so I can call?"

"Sure, step in and I'll get it for you."

"Ooh, you have a beautiful home here too."

"Thank you, Annie. We love it here. We're back off the main road, we have good neighbors and all the houses here are quite new and well maintained. Here is their number, Annie. Their names are Ted and Julie Wright."

"Thank you Donna, I'll speak to Tom about it and maybe give them a call."

"Okay, good luck Annie."

"Thanks again. Bye bye."

Annie took one more look as she drove by. *"Can't wait to see the inside."* She drove on home and started the task of fixing dinner for Tom. It would be an easy dinner tonight, shake and bake chicken and a tossed salad. Just throw it in the oven and put together a salad. Simple enough. Annie then poured two glasses of lemonade, grabbed the bag of cookies and the paper, and headed for the picnic table.

Tom soon arrived, a little dirty, as usual, and joined Annie at the table. With a kiss on the cheek he asked, "How was your day, honey?"

"I had a good day. How about you?"

"Good day, got a lot done. Everyone's happy, that's the main thing."

"Good, I baked you fresh cookies for you to have with your lemonade today."

"I see, honestly Annie I don't know how you do it day after day. You must get help from an elf or two. If not for the baking at least for the package you put them in."

"They've been known to give me a hand a time or two."

"So what do I owe this special treatment to?"

"I drove by a house today."

"That's an open-ended statement. Is there anything special about this house you drove by?"

Annie chuckled. "This house is coming up for sale, silly."

Tom smiled at her. "Okay, now you have my attention, tell me more."

"Well, I don't have a lot to tell. It's a three-bedroom, two-bath with a west-facing porch. Oh, and a big garage. I drove by and got their name and number so we can call and maybe make an appointment to take a look."

Tom sipped on his lemonade then took a couple bites on a cookie and said nothing. Annie just looked at him and finally said, "Well, what do you think?"

"I think you'd better pour the milk."

Annie jumped up and said, "POUR THE MILK,?" Slapped Tom on the shoulder, "You brat!" Tom laughed, "Payback!"

"Yeah, I know," said Annie, laughing, "It's a bitch. You sit still, Tom. I'll get the milk!"

Tom chuckled, got up and grabbed his cookies and lemonade and followed Annie into the house. He put the cookies and lemonade on the counter and threw his arms around Annie. She laughed, "I'm still mad at you."

Tom kissed Annie on the neck, "Sorry, I couldn't resist it. Is dinner about ready?"

"In about ten minutes, if you'd like to take a shower."

"Okay, thanks. I'll hurry." Tom took his shower and changed his clothes. He walked to the kitchen just as Annie was putting dinner on the table.

"I called the Wrights while you were in the shower to see if we could come over to take a look. I explained that Donna Thompson said they were thinking of putting their house on the market. Mrs. Wright asked if we could give her a few minutes to pick up. I told her we hadn't had our dinner yet, so would an hour or so be okay. She said that would be fine." Annie placed the chicken on the table, looked at Tom and asked, "What do you think? Never mind. I'll get the milk." Tom chuckled as Annie turned and walked to the refrigerator.

Tom stood and gave Annie a big hug, "I love you Annie." She put her arms around Tom's neck and said, "I love you too, even though you're a pain in the ass!"

After dinner Tom helped Annie pick up the kitchen. It wasn't hard to see that she was filled with anticipation. They wasted no time putting everything away. Then they jumped into the truck and headed south through Adams Center to Horner Drive. Tom parked his truck in front of house number 19.

"Wow, this is nice Annie!"

"I know, and I can't wait to see the inside." As they walked up the sidewalk Julie Wright came out onto the porch.

"Hello, I'm Julie," she said as she offered her hand. Tom and Annie graciously returned the introduction. "Please, come inside."

They entered a small vestibule just inside the front door, a closet and a half-wall planter that separated it from the living room. Opposite the living room was a formal dining room. They walked through, then on into the kitchen. The kitchen sink and window faced the west and the front of the house. The east wall had a picture window overlooking the back-yard. In front of the window was a breakfast booth. Beyond the kitchen to the south was an attached four-stall garage big enough for Tom to work in. If that weren't enough, the house had a full cellar that remained dry all year.

Walking through the living room and down the hall, a bath-room was on the right and a laundry room on the left. Also on the left were two nice sized bedrooms with ample closet space. On the right was the master bedroom with a master bath. The master bedroom had a huge closet, a make-up desk and plenty of room for a comfortable chair for reading.

"You have a wonderful home here. Why do you want to sell, if I may ask?"

"Well Annie my husband has been transferred west to over-see the construction of a new refinery there. He works for a major oil company. My husband was working in the Syracuse area and commuting from here every day, which wasn't bad.

But way out West -- that's just asking too much. So we've decided to make the change and move with him."

"Can you tell us about the taxes and the utility costs?"

"Yes I can Tom, I have put together a list of all the house expenses. If there is anything I have forgotten I would be happy to look that up for you."

"Thank you very much. Do you have any questions Tom?"

"Just one, What are you looking for price-wise?"

"Well, if you are interested, we are prepared to make you this offer. We have not called a realtor yet, so we do not have that expense. We were thinking of asking $52,000. The realtor's commission would be $3,640. If you have $3,000 more it would look like you have a $6,640 down payment, which is well above the 10% required to buy a home. Plus closing costs, of course. The only catch is that we must know if you are interested within, shall we say, seven days. After that we would put it in the hands of a realtor."

"Wow, that's very generous of you," Annie said.

"Well, Donna Thompson speaks very highly of you both, and it's a win-win for all concerned."

"Let me promise you this," Tom said. "We WILL let you know one way or the other before the seven days have elapsed."

"Thank you," Annie said. "It's been a pleasure meeting you, Julie."

"The pleasure was mine."

Tom and Annie walked to the truck. Tom opened his door and Annie slid in. Tom slid in, closed the door and started the engine. "Would you like to go to Lillie's for desert?"

"Sure."

They drove to Lillie's and Tom held the door as Annie walked in. Lillie was quick to welcome them. "Coffee, Tom?"

"Two please Lillie!" Tom and Annie took a table in the back so they could talk.

Lillie place the coffee on their table. "What brings you two out this time of day?"

"We went for a short drive after dinner, and just decided we hadn't seen you in a couple of days so we stopped in," Tom teased.

"Oh you liar, but keep it coming." They all chuckled as Lillie slapped Tom on the shoulder. "Can I get you anything else?"

"What's the status on pie tonight?"

"We have all the regulars. Apple, blueberry, cherry, cheese cake, and two cream pies one black and one white. What's your pleasure?"

Annie looked at Tom, "Apple sounds good to me."

"We'll have two apple Lillie."

"Two apple it is. ORDER!"

"I like that house Tom!"

"There's a real problem Annie."

Annie lifted her eye brows, sat up straight. "What problem?"

With a big smile. "I like it too."

"Oh, whew, you had me for a second there."

"We have to put it together in seven days. We have the savings Annie, that's no problem. But we have to secure a mortgage and you know what they say! 'These things take time!'"

Annie said, "I can stop at the bank tomorrow and talk to someone about it if you want, and maybe get an application."

"The quicker the better. But this is a big step Annie. Are we ready?"

"I think so Tom. I think it's a good deal and we love the house. It's everything we're looking for."

"Okay then, let's give it our best shot."

It was just five days later and the mortgage was approved. Tom and Annie called Julie with the good news. Julie seemed to be pleased that they were able to get it all together.

Ted and Julie Wright were all packed up and ready to head west right after the closing, in just forty-five days. It took Tom and Annie just four hours to move in. They really didn't have a lot to move. The house seemed huge without all the furniture the Wrights had. Over the years it slowly filled up. *"We called it our labor of love,"* Tom thought, as he sat on the porch that Annie had loved so much.

# Annie's Ashes

## Chapter Thirteen

*I*t was Thursday morning. Tom rolled out of bed at his usual five a.m. He sat on the edge of his bed and rubbed his eyes, stood up and staggered into the bathroom. He brushed his teeth and threw some cold water in his face. *"Wow, that will wake anyone up,"* he thought. Tom dressed in his running attire and stepped outside. After a few stretches, he broke into a trot and headed for downtown and his usual running route. Five miles, just like always.

Tom returned home feeling good. He jumped into the shower and dressed for work. *"It's time, time to put my mind back where it belongs."* He went to the telephone and called David Willard. The phone rang twice and David answered.

"David Willard."

"David, Tommy Blake here."

"Yes Tom, how are you?"

"I'm good. Thought I'd come to work today."

"Sure, glad to have you. I put all of your tools in the construction trailer. You have a key, right?"

"Yes, it's on my key ring I'll be there a little before eight."

"That sounds good. I'll be looking for you."

Tom hung up the phone, made sure the house was locked and left through the garage. He slid onto the seat of his truck, started the engine then hit the garage door button. Tom then backed out of his driveway and headed for Lillie's Diner.

Tom entered the diner and waved to Lillie.

"Good morning Tom. It's good to see you." Lillie came to his table with a cup of coffee. "Are you headed to work, Tom?

"Yes, I've got to put my mind back to business."

"It'll be good for you Tom, you'll see. What can I get for you?"

"How about just a bagel and butter?"

"You've got it. ORDER!"

Tom sipped his coffee and just looked out the window. Soon he heard the cook yell, "ORDER UP." And Lillie brought him his bagel.

With something in his stomach besides coffee, Tom headed out the door. "Thanks Lillie, it's on the table."

"Okay Tom, have a good day."

"Will too."

Work was a welcome change. It took his mind off Annie. All of the men welcomed him back and avoided the Annie subject. By noontime Tom was actually hungry. He jumped into his truck and drove to the local Seven-Eleven and grabbed a sandwich and pint of milk. That actually tasted good. It put a little power in his punch. All in all, Tom felt like it was a good day.

Later, headed for home Tom thought it would be easier just to pull into Lillie's for dinner. When he walked through the door Lillie yelled, "Well, Tom, how was your day?"

"It was a welcome change, Lillie. What's the special?"

"Meatloaf, mashed potatoes with carrots and a drink. What do you think?"

"That sounds good to me."

"ONE SPECIAL PLEASE. What to drink, Tom?"

"Give me just a glass of water, would you please?"

"You've got it, Tom." Lillie brought Tom his water and the newspaper. "How about a little reading material while you wait, Tom?"

"Yeah, that sounds good."

"ORDER UP!" yelled the cook and Lillie brought Tom his dinner. "What is the crew working on?"

"The crew I was with today is up on Pheasant Run. We're putting up a new home for a couple out of Syracuse. They're relocating here because of Fort Drum."

"What's he into, do you know?"

"I'm not really sure; something to do with the military."

"Enjoy your dinner, Tom."

After dinner Tom asked Lillie what he owed her.

"It' seven-fifty with tax."

He left ten dollars on the table and waved as he headed for the door. "Thanks Tom!"

Tom jumped in his truck and headed for home. *"I think the first thing I'll do is mow that lawn. It hasn't been done in awhile."* He drove into the driveway and lifted the garage door. The lawnmower was sitting against the back wall. Tom checked the oil and filled it up with gas and proceeded to mow the lawn. When that was finished he needed a shower. Tom entered the kitchen from the garage and noticed the message light blinking on the phone. *"That can wait. I'll take my shower first."*

After a quick shower and a clean change of clothes he was feeling pretty good. He went to the phone and played the message back. "Hello Tom. This is Raymond Weldon at the funeral home. I just want you to know that your wife's body was released yesterday. We took her to the crematorium and have her ashes here, ready for you to pick up anytime. I'll be waiting for your call."

Tom noticed that all at once the house seemed cold and empty. He almost slipped back into a depressed state. Shaking it off, he grabbed the phone and dialed the funeral home.

A very soft voice spoke. "Weldon Funeral Home."

"Mr. Weldon?"

"Yes, this is Raymond Weldon."

"Tom Blake on this end."

"Yes, Mr. Blake."

"I got your message. When would be a good time for me to pick up my wife's ashes?"

"Whatever time is good for you, Mr. Blake."

"Shall we say fifteen to twenty minutes?"

"That would be fine. I'll be looking for you."

Tom left the house and got into Annie's car and drove into Adams, then down North Park Street to the funeral home. He pulled into the driveway and parked the car. Raymond Weldon opened the door and welcomed Tom into his office.

"It's been a beautiful day, Mr. Blake."

"Yes it has. We can use a few more just like it."

The urn with Annie's ashes was on Mr. Weldon's desk. It was a beautiful brass urn, engraved with Annie's full name, date of birth and date of death. Tom's eyes began to well up when Raymond handed it to him. "It's beautiful, Mr. Weldon. Thank you so much for your care and concern. I do appreciate it. I won't forget everything you have done for me, and for Annie. Thanks again."

"You're very welcome Tom. Take care."

Tom placed Annie's urn on the passenger's seat and headed for home. He walked into the kitchen, placed the urn on the breakfast booth table Then to the fridge for a picture of lemonade and a glass from the cupboard. He returned to the breakfast booth and talked to Annie and cried.

After a good cry, Tom continued to talk as if she was right there. "Where would you like to be, Annie? We have so many places that have such fond memories. Places that we've been to together, and special places: Lakeview, where I asked you to marry me; Talcott Falls, where we were married, and the last place that both our families were all together; Wanakena, where you took me on my very first camping trip; Cascade Mountain, our very first High Peak in our quest to become Forty-Sixers. It was so beautiful up there, remember? We didn't want to come down. Maybe that's the place. I'll spread your ashes on top of Cascade Mountain where our quest began."

Tom went to the TV and hit the power button. The screen lit up and he changed the channel to 214, the weather channel. He watched until the forecast with the weekend weather came on. "It will be clear and mild for all of Upstate New York, from Friday straight through till Monday evening. Then you can expect a few scattered showers," the weather announcer said.

*"That sounds good. I'll drive up Friday after work. Maybe I'll rent one of the cabins Annie and I stayed at on our honeymoon."*

Tom looked on the table for their photo album. It wasn't there. *"I just saw it the other day. I took some pictures out of it for Annie's collage."* The collage was leaning up against the wall near the kitchen. Tom looked it over and said, "There it is!" It was a picture of the two of them on their honeymoon at the Tail O' the Pup Cabins near Lake Placid.

Tom grabbed the phone and called information.

"Information, can I help you?"

"Yes, I need a number for Tail O' the Pup Cabins near Lake Placid."

"Yes, that number is…" Tom grabbed a pen and jotted down the number. "Thank you."

"You're welcome sir." Tom hung up the phone. He opened up his wallet and laid his credit card on the counter. Picked up the phone and dialed the number.

"Tail O' the Pup Cabins, can I help you?"

"I hope so. My name is Tom Blake. I'd like to make a reservation for this weekend if I could."

"Sure, no problem. When do you expect to arrive?"

"Not before nine o'clock Friday night. Is that a problem?"

"No sir that would be fine. And how many nights do you expect to stay?"

"Two nights, Friday and Saturday."

"Okay. And a credit card number?"

Tom read the number and the person on the other end said, "This is your confirmation number, sir." Tom jotted it down and placed it in his wallet with his credit card.

"Are we all set?"

"You're all set, sir. Thank you."

Tom hung up the phone. Next morning he got up at his usual 5:00 a.m. and went for his usual five mile run. It was a habit he didn't want to forget. It cleared his mind and made him feel good about himself. After his run he took a shower and got ready for work.

Tom placed his hand on Annie's urn as he walked by, headed for his truck. With the house locked up, he headed for Lillie's Diner.

Lillie greeted him as he came through the door. "Morning, Tom. Headed for the job?"

"Yeah, it looks like it'll be a great day, don't you think Lillie? A let's git-er-done kind of day."

"That's the spirit Tom! What can I get you this morning?"

"Coffee and that plain bagel with just butter should do me this morning."

"You've got it. ORDER!"

Lillie brought Tom his coffee and the newspaper. "This will get you started."

Tom glanced through the paper until he heard the cook yell, "ORDER UP!" and Lillie delivered his bagel. "There you go Tom. Enjoy."

"Thanks Lillie. While you're here, what do I owe you?"

"Three-fifty with tax."

Tom finished his coffee and bagel, left a five dollar bill on the table and waved to Lillie as he left.

"Have a good day, Tom!"

It was a good day on the job. Everything was a fast pace. The weather was perfect and the day went as planned. Tom took a short break for lunch and spoke with David Willard.

"I'm planning to take Annie's ashes to the mountains this weekend. I should to be back Sunday night or Monday at the latest, if that's alright."

"No problem, Tom. You do what you have to."

"And if you don't mind, David, this is just between you and me. I don't want the men avoiding me because they don't know what to say."

"Understood, Tom. And again, you take all the time you need."

"Thanks, Dave."

Tom finished out the day and locked everything in the construction trailer. Then he yelled to the men to have a good weekend, jumped in his truck and headed for home. He opened the garage door as he pulled into the drive. With the door fully open he drove into the garage. Tom entered the kitchen and placed his hand on Annie's urn as he walked by. There were no messages on the phone and only junk in the mail box.

After his shower, Tom threw a few things in an overnight bag and put it in the back seat of Annie's car. He made one more trip to place her urn in the front seat. Backing the car out of the garage, he decided to let Bob and Donna Thompson know that he'd be gone for a few days. Tom took Annie's house key off her key ring and walked over to the Thompson's. After he knocked on the door, Donna answered by opening it.

"Oh hello, Tom. What's up?"

"Hi, Donna. I'm going away for a few days and I'd like you to kind of keep an eye on the place while I'm gone, if you would."

"Sure Tom, no problem. Is everything alright?"

"Everything is fine. Here's a key to the front door, if you need to get in for any reason. I should be back on Sunday, Monday at the latest."

"Okay Tom. Be careful."

"I will. Thanks, Donna."

Driving through Adams Center, he decided not to stop at Lillie's Diner for a bite to eat. *"I'll stop in Harrisville, there's a diner there that we always stop at on our way through."* Tom made the Rose Garden Diner in just an hour and a half. He walked through the door and sat at a table for two in the back. A young waitress looked around the corner, smiling, and asked, "Coffee?"

"Please, and a glass of water."

"Cream and sugar?"

"Just black, thanks."

The waitress brought Tom his coffee and water, told him that the special was a fish sandwich with macaroni and cheese.

"Yeah, that sounds good. And some tartar sauce, please."

"Sure thing!"

After finishing his dinner, he left two dollars on the table and walked to the register. "What are the damages ma'am?"

"Eight-fifty with tax."

With change in hand, Tom waved and walked out the door. Annie's car was in the parking lot across the street. He slid in under the steering wheel and was soon back on the road headed northeast, driving over familiar roads to Star Lake, Cranberry Lake, Tupper, and Saranac Lakes. He drove through Lake Placid, then turned right onto Route 73. A couple of miles ahead on the right he saw Tail O' the Pup Cabins. *"This is where Annie and I stayed on our honeymoon, that Columbus Day weekend."*

Tom checked in and to his surprise received the key to the same cabin they had on their wedding night. Tom parked Annie's car in front of their cabin, turned off the engine and just sat, remembering back.

What a wonderful weekend that was. It was about six thirty when we checked in, and it was about time for dinner. I noticed a nice restaurant back in Lake Placid. "We can have our first dinner as husband and wife there if you like, Annie?"

We drove the short distance back to The Lake Placid Inn and Restaurant for an enchanting dinner in a quiet corner, with a fireplace flickering its dance on the ceiling. The mood was one of love and romance. Annie had never looked as beautiful as she did on that special day. After dinner we stayed and listened to the band playing in the bar. *"I held her tight in my arms as we danced to a couple of slow tunes. Then we returned to our cabin, where we made love on into the night."*

Next morning we arose around six, showered and dressed for our first High Peaks climb. We drove on into Keene, to a small diner called ADK Café. After a wonderful breakfast and two coffees to go, we drove to the trail head. The sign read that it was a 2.4-mile trail and had an almost two thousand foot elevation change. That's a twenty percent grade any day of the week.

We headed down the trail and registered at the registration box at 7:30 a.m. We were excited, to say the least. The trail was rough, with big boulders to climb over most of the way. Shortly after starting, the aroma of fall leaves was in the air. What a wonderful smell. Later balsam fir passed through our senses.

We climbed steadily and kept hydrated to avoid muscle cramps. We came to a small opening in the tree line. I turned around and was struck by the wonderful view of fall colors, mountains and valleys. "Oh, my God, Annie! Take a look at this!" She stood by my side. "Oh Tom isn't it beautiful?"

"It sure is. Just look at the color. This is beauty I can't find words to describe." We looked for just a minute, then turned to get higher and see even more.

Just about 8:30 the sun began to peek through the trees. We continued to climb on up to a bigger and better overlook. Here the trees opened up to a clear view of the tapestry that lay before us. We sat for awhile, my arm around Annie's shoulder, just holding her close and loving every moment.

Eventually we stood and continued up. There were flat sections but few and short. The climb went steadily up. Before the summit, we passed the junction to Porter Mountain. We would take that trail on our way down. Not long after, the tree line opened up and the summit was in sight. A yellow-painted dotted trail marked the way to the summit, to avoid walking on the fragile plant life on the summit. We followed the markings to the top and found the benchmark. Annie was all smiles when we hit the top. I gave her a great big hug and a quick kiss. "One down. Only forty-five to go."

She turned to look and gasped at the sheer beauty that lay three hundred and sixty degrees around us.

It had taken us an hour and thirty minutes to make our first climb. We sat at the top and munched on a few cookies and drank some water. After about an hour we started down. At the top we had had the summit all to ourselves. We met our first company close to the junction of Porter Mountain. It was only seven-tenths of a mile to the summit; a short descent then a steady ascent to a tree covered summit with no real overlook.

We made the short hike and had to look for the benchmark. "That's two, Annie. Forty-four to go."

The decent back down was harder on the knees than the climb up. It was important to remain in shape. It made the experience so much more enjoyable.

We were back to the car by one o'clock, and hungry. First on the agenda was lunch. We went back into Lake Placid, stopped at a fast food hamburger place and had a quick bite to eat. After lunch we walked the streets of Lake Placid. What a wonderful little town. It held the 1932 and the 1980 Winter Olympic Games. We spent the entire afternoon walking and looking in the shops.

Tom woke up at five a.m., rolled out of bed and rubbed his eyes. He decided to take a shower and get ready for the day. He dressed for the hike, including his boots, filled a couple water bottles and placed Annie in his day pack. He locked his cabin, slid in under the wheel and started the car. He turned right out of the driveway and checked on the ADK Café. It was still there and still open. Tom was the first customer of the day.

"Good morning, sir. What can I get you?"

"How about a plain bagel with butter and a coffee?"

"Sure thing. It looks like it's going to be a beautiful day."

"Yes, it does. Can I get a club sandwich to go also?"

"Not a problem."

The bagel hit the spot. The gentleman gave Tom his sandwich in a to-go box and asked if there was anything else.

"A black coffee to go would be great."

"Are you hiking today, sir?"

"Yes, I'm going to the top of Cascade."

"It's a good day for it. It should be clear on top."

"I hope so. I love it up there."

"You're starting early enough. You should have it to your-self for a while. It's a popular spot. You'll see quite a few people late morning to early afternoon."

"Guess I'd better get going then. Thanks again."

"You have a wonderful day, sir."

Tom paid the tab, waved as he walked out the door. He drove the short ten minute drive to the trail head, then parked the car. Tom donned his day pack, clipped on his water bottles and headed down to the register box. As he signed in he thought, *"I'm the first climber of the day."*

Then he headed up. It was a familiar climb. He turned to look, as they had done together. He paused for an occasional drink and sat at the large overlook. Then he climbed on up until the trees opened up with the summit in sight. It took him just an hour and a half to cover 2.4 miles, with an ascent of almost two thousand feet.

Tom sat on the summit all by himself, holding Annie close to his heart. *"Here we are again Annie, on the top of Cascade Mountain. This is where our quest to become Forty-Sixers began. I know you'll be happy here in your beloved high peaks. We almost climbed them all. Whiteface, Algonquin, Dix, Haystack. All but one, Marcy, the tallest one of all, fifty-two hundred feet above sea level. That is the only one stopping us from becoming Forty-Sixers. Why did this have to happen? We were so close. So close to our goal."*

Tom's eyes began to well up as he talked to Annie sitting on the summit. *"We were almost there. One more climb, that's all it would have taken."* The tears were flowing holding Annie close, it was just the two of them, alone in the High Peaks. Tom, with his eyes filled with tears sat up straight and yelled.

"I CAN'T DO IT! I CAN'T DO IT! Not here. No not here anyway. We're going to finish. I'm taking you to the top of Mount Marcy. We WILL become Forty-Sixers, Annie. I made you a promise and I'm going to keep it!"

Tom placed Annie back into his day pack and headed down with a new agenda in mind. This one, he was sure, was the right choice. He had a definite smile on his face and knew he had made the right decision for his heart. There was a livelier step in his pace. Tom was back at the car in record time.

*"Okay, Annie where do we go? Where is the trail head to Marcy?"* Checking their trails book for the High Peaks region, Tom researched several routes to the summit of Marcy. The shortest route was 7.4 miles one way.

*"Oh Annie, this is going to take some planning. There is no way I can hike almost fifteen miles in one day, with an ascent of 3166 feet. I'll have to camp over night. According to the book the last available campsite is 2.3 miles from Heart Lake. What we should do is drive to Heart Lake and park the car there, pack in the 2.3 miles to a campsite and make a base camp there. Next day we'll make the climb to the summit and spread your ashes, return to the base camp, which would be about a ten mile hike. With the extreme elevation*

*change on that day, carrying only a day pack, I think to do it in one day would be asking too much."*

Turning around, Tom drove back toward North Elba and turned onto the Adirondack Loj Road. Driving in about five miles, he arrived at the High Peaks Information Center and Heart Lake, with its large parking lot. *"Okay, we know where we have to go. Hopefully next weekend the weather will cooperate and we'll get it done."*

It was getting late in the afternoon, so Tom decided to go into Keene and stop at the ADK Café for a bite to eat before making the long drive home. He was welcomed back when he walked through the door.

"How was your climb, sir?"

"It was a good climb, a beautiful day for it. The sky was clear and the view, endless."

"Glad to hear it. Can I get you anything?"

"Yeah, do you have a special?"

"We sure do -- a hot turkey sandwich with French fries."

"That's a little too much for me. Can I get just the hot turkey with a glass of water?"

"You sure can. I'll have it ready in a snap."

Tom was just finishing his sandwich when the gentleman asked, "Can I get you anything else, sir?"

"How about a black coffee to go?"

"No problem. You say you're headed home?"

"Yes, Adams Center is where I come from."

"What's that, about three hours from here?"

"Yes, just about."

"Well, drive carefully. Hope to see you again."

"As a matter of fact, if the weather cooperates I'll be back next weekend. I like your establishment, I'll be sure to stop in."

"I'll be looking for you, sir. Take care."

Tom paid the bill and waved as he walked out the door.

His next stop was Tail O' the Pup Cabins. Tom picked up the cabin and put everything in his overnight bag. At the office, the manager asked, "Checking out?"

"Yeah, my trip got cut a little short. I'll pay for both nights if it's a problem."

"No problem, sir. Just the one night is sixty-five, plus an even five dollars tax."

Tom paid with cash and said, "See you next time," and walked out the door.

Sliding in under the wheel, Tom started the car and headed back toward Lake Placid. It was such a small narrow town that you need both hands on the wheel as you drive through. Past the town now, Tom started sipping on his coffee and he pointed the car for home.

Tom arrived home at about six o'clock. He put his day pack on the floor and placed Annie back on the breakfast booth table. *"I'll start putting things together for next weekend right after I start a load of laundry and take a shower."* With the laundry started and shower taken. He started getting things out of the spare bedroom: tent, sleeping bag, change of clothes, three pairs of socks, (from lessons learned), sweats to sleep in, cooking utensils, freeze-dried food, instant coffee, compass and GPS, flashlight and a small roll of TP. *"That's a start, I'll probably think of more as I start packing it all together."*

Tom returned to the kitchen, poured himself a glass of water and sat at the table with Annie. He talked to her as he mapped out his route to Mount Marcy from Heart Lake, using his trail book and topo maps. *"My biggest concern, Annie, is a campsite. If they're full, it's a turnaround back to Marcy Dam for a site. Keep your fingers crossed."*

On Sunday morning Tom got up at his usual time, put on his jogging clothes and did a few stretches before starting his trot. *"I'll do the usual four miles, then sprint the last mile. That gets the old heart pumping."*

After his run he slowed to a walk in front of the house.

Tom needed a shower and a change of clothes, but first he put on the coffee. Tom was completely refreshed and felt good as he poured his first cup and sat with Annie at the breakfast booth.

*"What to do today, Annie? I'll get my back pack all set for next weekend. That won't take long. I all most forgot. I need to throw*

*the laundry in to the dryer. The laundry is something you always did. That and keeping the house picked up. I guess I've been letting things go lately. Yeah, thanks Annie. I'll do all those things today. That'll be a good job well done."*

After just one cup he started right in. Cloths in the dryer. Then put the dirty dishes in the dishwasher and got it started. Next he got out the vacuum cleaner and pushed that around. He did a second load of laundry, sheets and pillow cases, then he emptied the dishwasher and put the dishes away. With all that done, Tom sat with Annie and a second cup of coffee. *"What's next?"* he wondered. He looked at Annie's urn and said, *"Yep, you're right, I am bored out of my mind. I guess I could sweep out the garage, then what? It's not even noon yet. What on earth will I do the rest of the day?"*

With the work all done, Tom decided to walk over to the Thompson's. Maybe they would have some coffee. He walked next door and rang the door bell. Bob answered the door.

"Hi Tom. We didn't expect you back so soon."

"I had a change of plans and came back early. Say, have you got any coffee?"

"Yes, I sure do. Come on in."

They walked into the kitchen and sat at the table. Donna came in.

"Oh hi, Tom. What's going on today?"

"I just thought I'd bother you two for a coffee."

Donna chuckled, "You're no bother. Come over anytime."

Bob poured the three cups, with three spoons for cream and sugar. Before Donna sat down she said, "Let me get your key, Tom."

"No, that's okay. You hang on to it. I plan on a return trip next weekend, weather permitting."

"A return trip? Where are you returning to?"

"I was up in the Adirondacks and I didn't get done what I was planning, so I've got to go back. Hopefully next time I'll get it done."

"Sounds mysterious, Tom. You're not planning on moving away or anything are you?"

"No, it's nothing like that, just some unfinished business to take care of. I'll tell you all about it when it's done."

"Don't get us wrong. We're not trying to be nosy, just making conversation, Donna explained. Tom chuckled.

They drank two cups of coffee each and Tom said, "Well, I've bothered you two enough for one day. Thanks for the coffee."

"Any time. Don't be a stranger."

"Thanks again." Tom headed for home.

The rest of the afternoon was spent packing his backpack for next weekend. With everything in its proper place, the pack tipped the scales at just thirty-nine pounds. *"That's an easy load, I'll carry that to the campsite then take just my daypack to the top."*

On Monday morning Tom rolled out of bed at five a.m., like every other day, put on his jogging clothes, did a few stretches, and then took off for his five-mile run. It was just six o'clock when Donna went to the kitchen to get water to make coffee. She saw Tom returning from his run, up the front steps to the door. Donna turned from the window and quickly turned back. *"Did I see what I think I saw?"* She looked across the front yard and caught Tom walking into his house. *"I swear I saw the young woman on his front porch! No, I'm not going there again! I didn't see anything."*

Work was especially good for Tom at this point. With his mind on the job, he wasn't thinking about Annie. At home, that's all he thought about. The house was too quiet so he made himself busy in the shop. One night it was a bird feeder for the back yard. Another night it was shelves for the garage. And so on went the week. Soon it was Saturday morning and time to load up and head to the Adirondack Park.

It was a beautiful morning. The forecast was warm and mild with just a slight chance of rain. There was a lump in Tom's throat as he placed Annie on the front seat of the car. *"This is it, Annie. Here we go."* With the house all locked up and the garage door down, he started the car and backed out the driveway.

Harrisville was the first stop at just about 9:00 a.m.

"Good morning, sir. What can I get you today?"

"Good morning. Just a plain bagel with butter and a black coffee please."

"Sure thing." The waitress brought Tom his coffee.

"It's a beautiful day, sir. Are you headed into the Park?"

"Yeah, just going camping. I may climb a mountain if the spirit moves me." And he smiled.

"Sounds like the weather will be perfect for that."

Tom finished his bagel, left a dollar tip on the table and walked to the counter.

"Could I have a black coffee to go, please?"

"Sure thing."

Tom paid the bill, said "Thank you very much." and walked out the door. He was on the road again, driving through Star Lake, Cranberry, Tupper and Saranac. Tom soon reached Lake Placid. It was just 12:30. *"I may as well stop at the ADK Café for some lunch before heading into Heart Lake."*

Tom turned onto Route 73 and headed for Keene. He parked the car in the lot and walked into the café.

"Good afternoon, sir. I see you made it back."

"Yes, the weather looks really good for the weekend so I thought I'd come back and get-it-done, if you know what I mean."

"Sounds like you have a plan, sir."

"I'd like to summit Mount Marcy this weekend."

That's great. I expect it's going to be clear on top all weekend for you."

"I hope so! What's a climb without the view?"

"I hear you, sir. What can I get you?"

"That pork Bar-B-Q sounds good, with a glass of water. And no fries please."

"Right away, sir."

"After lunch, can I get a bottle of water to go, please? And what do I owe you?"

"It comes to just seven dollars with tax."

Tom gave him the seven dollars, left a two dollar tip.

"It was excellent. Thank you very much."

"You're welcome. Have a good climb. Stop in on your way back!"

"I'll do that. Thank you very much." Tom waved and walked to the car.

Soon he was on the road to Heart Lake. Tom placed his hand on Annie's urn. "Almost there." He drove the five miles into Heart Lake, then parked the car. He removed his backpack from the trunk and placed Annie in the top and closed it up. He shut the trunk and stood his backpack on it and slid his arms into the shoulder straps. He hooked his waist belt and his chest strap, looked over his shoulder. "Ready, Annie, here we go."

The sign-in register was at the end of the parking lot. Tom signed in: Destination? Mt. Marcy. Length of stay? Three days. Number in party? Two. He closed the register and headed down the trail. The lean-to and campsite at Heart Lake were occupied and the parking lot was over half full, making Tom a little nervous about getting the campsite he wanted. When they had gone close to a half mile, they crossed Algonquin Brook.

After one mile they turned left and headed for Marcy Dam. The hike was easy and the pitch was gentle. At a little over two miles they came to and crossed The Dam. Tom stopped on the dam for a short pause and took in the views of Phelps and Golden Mountains and Algonquin Peak. All the lean-tos and campsites around this small body of water were taken.

At the end of the dam there was another register. Again Tom registered as a party of two. Just up the trail about fifty yards was the DEC Interior Outpost at Marcy Dam. At the trail register they turned right and hooked up with the Van Hovenberg Trail about a hundred yards later. Bearing left, they followed the trail on the bank of the Phelps Brook. They followed the brook and came to the campsite Tom wanted to stay at. They walked into an empty site. "Oh my god, Annie, its empty. I thought for sure someone would be here."

Tom was quick about shedding his backpack and taking Annie out and placing her on the top. He pulled out his package of cookies, unsnapped his bottle of water and sat on his butt, leaning against the same tree Annie was against. He took a much needed break, munching on cookies and sipping on water before he started setting up camp. Tom set Annie on the ground when he pulled out the tent, sleeping bag and paraphernalia for dinner.

The tent was flat on the ground and Tom had started threading the poles through the sleeves when he stopped, looked at Annie and said with a smile, *"Are you just going to sit there or are you going to help?"* Then he laughed. *"Never mind, I'll do it. You can cook dinner. No? Uh, okay, I'll do that too."* After finishing with the tent, he spread out his sleeping bag. *"There, that's done. Now, what's for dinner? I think I'll have one of my favorites, Chili Mac."* Tom put water on to boil for his dinner while sipping on his bottle of water. After the water boiled, he fixed his dinner.

Tom nibbled away on his dinner and talked to Annie. *"I'll finish my dinner then go to bed early. I want to hit the trail at first light tomorrow and be the first to summit. I hope we'll have the summit to ourselves for a while."* After dinner he changed into his sweats, crawled into the tent and slid into his sleeping bag.

Tom woke up at five a.m., put water on to boil and changed into his hiking clothes and boots. While sipping on his coffee and nibbling on a few cookies he placed Annie in his day pack with the rest of the bag of cookies. With the pack on his back he took the last sip of coffee, looked over his shoulder. *"It's time to go, Annie,"* and they headed up the trail.

Shortly after leaving the camp they passed the junction to Phelps Mountain. At the bridge over Phelps Brook Tom stopped and refilled his water bottles using his water filter. After a couple of sips they were on the trail again. The trail seemed to make a steeper grade here and leveled off, with his first clear view of Mount Marcy, straight ahead. At the top of Indian Falls they stopped for a sip of water and admired the view of the MacIntyre Range.

The trail took several changes in elevation, some steep, some slight, along with some up and some down. They also passed other trail junctions with different destinations. Tom and Annie's destination remained the same, the summit of Mount Marcy. They passed several old lean-to sites where camping was no longer allowed.

The dome of Marcy was now in full view. The trail passed through some scrub brush, then opened up in the Arctic Zone. From this point on hikers had to walk on the painted trail to preserve the fragile vegetation. They continued on through the last bog and onto the first shoulder of Marcy, on the smaller Eastern summit. With the true summit in sight just a few hundred feet away Tom stopped, removed his day pack and took several deep breaths then sat on the ground. Now holding Annie.

*"This isn't right. We can't do it this way, Annie. I want you to wait for me here."* With that Tom stood, cast her ashes in a large, high semicircle. *"I'll be back later Annie, and I'll join you in the next life. We'll summit together, just like I promised ... together"*. Tom sat on the rock with tears in his eyes and pulled out a pad of paper and his GPS from his day pack. With the

unit ready to navigate, he set a waypoint as number 46 and began to write: "This is my final request."

With his task completed Tom stood and pulled on his day pack. *"I love you Annie. I'll always love only you. This is not good-bye, just, I'll be back later."* Tom turned and headed back down. He was still very emotional, wiping the tears from his eyes as he walked, trying not to look back. *"I've done what I've done. I only hope, I did it right."*

Tom kept a steady pace back down the mountain, the way they walked up, never stopping until he reached camp. It was just four o'clock. He shed his day pack and placed Annie's urn on top of his backpack. *"I need to fix myself some dinner. Cookies just haven't quite been enough today."* He put the water on to boil, pulled out his entrée, chili mac and prepared the proper amount of water to be boiled. He sat with his back against a tree, sipping his water, putting away his diner and feeling very alone. *"But I'm not alone, I have all my memories and I will always have them. I will spend the rest of my life remembering Annie and the things we've done, the places we've been and the things we've seen. I will never be alone!"*

In the morning Tom woke up at five. *"First things first. Coffee! Looks like it will be a beautiful day. The sky is clear and the wind is calm."* He started his coffee water and began the task of packing up. After packing away his sleeping bag and tent and putting everything back in its place on his pack, Tom sat and enjoyed his coffee. *"I'm really not hungry now. Maybe I'll* stop at the ADK Café for some lunch when I get back down. After that I should be set for the drive home."

With his cup packed away, he slipped into his shoulder straps, snapped his hip and chest straps. He made one more look around to be sure it looked the same way it did when they walked in, then headed out. The hike back to the car was effortless and the views were endless. *"There is so much to see, it just never gets old. The park changes with every season. What you're looking at today may change tomorrow. We always loved our time here in the mountains."*

Tom reached the car around eleven o'clock and started feeling hungry. Yes, lunch was definitely on his mind. He placed his pack in the trunk and Annie's urn on the passenger seat. He started the car and stopped at the gate to pay for the three days' parking, then headed for the café.

At 11:45, Tom walked through the door.

"Good morning, sir. How was your climb?"

"It was a good climb. I got done what I needed to get done. The top was clear and the view was endless."

"Good, I'm glad to hear it. Today's special is meatloaf with mashed potatoes and carrots. What do you think?"

"That sounds good. Go easy on the potatoes, if you would."

"Sure thing."

After lunch Tom asked what the damages were and paid the Seven dollar tab.

"Are you planning another trip up this way sir?"

"Oh, I'll be back. I just don't know exactly when. I'm sure you haven't seen the last of me." Tom left a dollar tip on the counter, waved and walked out the door. The three and a half hour drive home was uneventful. The only thing on Tom's mind was what to do with Annie's urn.

By the time he arrived home, he knew exactly what he was going to do. But first, he had to call his lawyer and change his living trust. He went into the kitchen to look up the phone number, then dialed.

"Hello, Johnson Law Firm."

"Yes, this is Thomas Blake. Is Mr. Johnson in?"

"One moment, Mr. Blake."

A moment later a man's voice said, "Yes Tom, what can I do for you?"

"Well, to start with, my wife has passed and I'd like to change my living trust."

"Oh Tom, I'm sorry for your loss. Do you know what you want to do?"

"Yes I do."

Okay, let me put you on "record." Now Tom, tell me who you are and exactly what you want done. I'll have it printed and sent to you tomorrow. Sign both copies, keep one for your records and mail the other back to the office." Sometime later, Tom finished explaining his wishes and hung up the phone.

He went straight to his work shop, pulled out some beautiful red oak and started in on his project. Tom turned out a beautiful small bench with a heart-shaped back, to sit on the breakfast booth table. In the center of the heart he recessed his favorite eight by ten picture of Annie. "Perfect!"

# Moving on

## Chapter Fourteen

On Tuesday morning, Tom rolled out of bed at his usual time, put on his jogging clothes and ran his usual five miles. He showered, got dressed for work and headed for Lillie's Diner.

"Good morning, Tom." Yelled Lillie when he came through the door.

"Morning, Lillie. Can I get a coffee and a bagel with butter, please?"

Lillie nodded her head and said, "ORDER!" She brought Tom his coffee and asked, "Where have you been hiding yourself? I haven't seen you for a while."

"I was up in the mountains for a few days, just clearing my head."

"Well, you're looking much better, Tom. Those mountains of yours must be good medicine."

"ORDER UP!" the cook yelled.

"I'll get your breakfast."

He finished his breakfast and got a coffee to go. "It's on the table Lillie," Tom yelled as he walked out the door.

When Tom got to the job he went straight to see David Willard.

"Morning, Tom."

"Morning, Dave. I just want to thank you for understanding about the time I needed. I finished what we talked about. I spread Annie's ashes in the mountains, although she and I had never talked about it. I'm sure I did what she would have wanted me to do."

David nodded his head and placed his hand on Tom's shoulder. "Are we ready to rumble?"

Tom smiled. "Let's get-it-done."

"All right!"

On Tuesday, work was great and everything when smoothly. Late Wednesday afternoon Tom started thinking about Annie. At dinner he decided he wanted to go back to Lakeview, where he had asked her to marry him. *"I'm not alone. I have my memories. And Annie is the last person I see before I leave the house and the first person I see when I get back home."*

When Tom left the diner he parked the truck in his driveway and thought about putting the canoe on the truck and going to Lakeview. *"Maybe I'll ask Bob Thompson if he would like to go. We could make better time in the canoe with the two of us paddling rather than just me."*

Tom walked over to the Thompson's and rang the bell. Donna answered the door. "Hi, Tom. Do you want your key?"

"No, that's okay. You hang on to it for me, if you don't mind."

"Okay, what's on your mind?"

"Is Bob home?"

"No, he's in Florida. He won't be back until sometime next week. What do you need?"

"Well, I was thinking about going to Lakeview Beach and wondered if he'd like to go and help paddle the canoe."

Donna smiled. "When are you doing that?"

"Right now!"

"Well, if I didn't have plans I'd go with you. I'm free tomorrow. Can you wait till then?"

"Yeah, tomorrow's good, as long as the weather cooperates. I'll check the forecast and let you know"

"You can check it here Tom."

"Are you sure? I don't want to impose."

"Don't be ridiculous. Step in."

Tom stepped through the door and kicked off his shoes just inside. Donna grabbed her laptop, took it to the kitchen and placed it on the table.

"Here Tom, you look up whatever you need. Can I get you something to drink?"

Tom opened the laptop. "A glass of water would be good, thanks." He checked weather info for upstate New York and clicked tomorrow's forecast. It called for mild temperatures, a slight breeze from the southwest and a mix of clouds and sun. "The weather sounds good. Have you ever paddled a canoe before Donna?"

"No, but is it going to kill me to learn?"

"I don't know. Can you swim?"

"Do I need to swim?"

"No, not as long as you sit still. A canoe is not something you can get up and walk around in."

"Well, I'll do whatever you tell me to do, how's that?"

Donna gave Tom a glass of ice water and they made idle chit chat about work, about Bob, and inevitably about Annie. Donna spoke about missing her at work, missing the time when they were on break laughing. How Annie made it a joy to go to work. "I don't ever remember her being in a bad mood Tom."

Tom smiled, "I know what you mean. She wasn't only my wife. She was and still is my very best friend. She just has trouble paddling the canoe." Donna laughed.

Tom finished his glass of water stood up to leave. "Thanks for the water. Are you sure you want to go to Lakeview with me tomorrow?"

"I do, if you can put up with my paddling."

"I'm sure you'll do fine. Bring a towel and wear your swim suit, in case you want to go for a swim. And a dry change would be a good idea."

"Okay, I will."

"Why don't you come over about 6:00 Donna. I'll have everything loaded and ready to go."

"Okay, Tom. I'll see you about six."

After he got home, Tom got out the paddles and the life jackets and a few tie-downs for the canoe. In the kitchen he checked the refrigerator for a couple of beers, a couple of sodas and two waters, not really knowing what Donna might want to drink. After that he checked his mail. There was an envelope from his lawyer. In it was his new living trust. Tom read it all over and signed both copies. He found a new envelope, addressed it back to his lawyer and put it out in the box for his carrier to pick up tomorrow.

Tom then got a ten by twelve manila envelope out and placed his will and his ADK logbook inside, with a cover letter. He licked the adhesive on the flap and sealed the envelope. With a magic marker he wrote on the face MY FINAL REQUEST. Then he pinned it over his bed. He retrieved his GPS unit from his backpack and hung it over his bed as well.

Next morning he went through his usual routine - up at five, go for a run, shower and dress for work. Stop at Lillie's Diner for a bagel and coffee, then hit the job. Work was keeping him sane at this point, keeping his mind active and not dwelling too much on the past. After work, his past with Annie is just about all he thought about.

"4:30, it's time to pick up, fellas!" The men put everything away in the construction trailer and locked up. Tom slid in under the wheel of his truck and headed for Lillie's. He entered the diner and sat at his usual table. Lillie looked over at Tom. "Water Tom?"

"If you would please Lillie."

Lillie delivered an ice cold glass of water and the paper. She placed them on Tom's table. "Chicken and biscuits with a tossed salad, Tom. What do you think?"

"Sounds good, Lillie. How about ranch dressing on my salad?"

"You've got it. ORDER!"

After dinner Tom paid the tap and left a tip on his table. Drove home, parked the truck in the drive and began loading the canoe, life jackets and paddles. With that job done, he went into the bedroom and put on his swim suit and grabbed a towel. Back in the kitchen he put the beer, soda and water in a small cooler. Then he sat with Annie and drank a bottle of water waiting for Donna to arrive about six o'clock.

Donna walked over and came to the kitchen door and knocked. Tom answered the door. "Donna, step in."

Donna entered the kitchen and noticed the bench with Annie's urn and picture on the table. "Oh Tom, did you make that?"

"Yes, I did."

"How clever! I've never seen anything like it before."

"It's just an idea that came to me on my way home from the mountains Monday."

"That's a good picture of Annie."

"It's my favorite. I put some drinks in a cooler in case we get thirsty. Is there anything else you can think of we might need?"

"I can't think of anything."

"Let's be gone then."

They jumped in the truck and backed out of the driveway. When they reached Route 11 he turned left.

"Where is this Lakeview, Tom?"

"It's down Route 3, west of Belleville. If you've never been in a canoe, you've never been to Lakeview, have you Donna?"

"No, I can't say that I have. Is there a reason you want to go there?"

"Well actually, there is. It's where I asked Annie to marry me when I was twenty-three years old. And since all I have are memories, I want to keep them alive and fresh in my mind. I want to be twenty-three again."

They drove down Route 3 and turned onto Pierrepont Place. The road ended after about a half mile at a parking lot and boat launch. They exited the truck. Donna grabbed her beach bag and the cooler and asked, "Where do we go, Tom?"

"Just over there. You'll see the boat ramp going into the water." Tom untied the canoe and slid it onto his shoulders and headed for the water. He put it down and then headed back for the paddles and life jackets. When he returned

Tom held out a life jacket. "Here Donna, put this on in case we go swimming before we want to." She put it on, made a slight adjustment and snapped the two clips together. Tom placed the cooler and Donna's beach bag in the canoe and asked Donna to get in the front of the canoe. He handed her a paddle and shoved off.

Tom hopped in the back, grabbed a paddle and headed for the beach, which was a good mile away. "All you have to do, Donna, is to reach out in front of you with the paddle and draw the water toward you."

"That's it?"

"Yup, and enjoy." They paddled south to the end of the pond, then into the outlet.

"This is kind of cool Tom. I've never done anything like this."

"Annie and I did stuff like this all the time: canoeing, backpacking, mountain climbing and some just plain camping."

"She used to tell me where you two had been when we had coffee at school."

They paddled on toward the lake. "Did you get done what you wanted to in the mountains over the weekend, Tom?"

"Yes, I did."

"Can you talk about it or would you rather not?"

"Yeah, sure, I'll tell you, but don't mind me if I get emotional. I took Annie's ashes to the mountains. Annie wanted to be a Forty-Sixer. That is, there are forty-six high peaks in the Adirondack Park, over four thousand feet high. If you climb them all, you become a Forty-Sixer.

We climbed them all but one, the highest one. We were in that area several times and could have climbed it at any time. But we wanted to save the biggest for the last. Then Annie died before we got it done. I promised her that we would be Forty-Sixers. So I took her up Mount Marcy last weekend."

"Did you spread her ashes on the summit?"

"No I couldn't. I stopped a few hundred feet from the top and spread her ashes there."

"You did! Why there?"

"Because when I die I want my ashes to be spread there as well. Then Annie and I can summit together in the next life."

"Oh Tom, I can honestly say," as tears began to form in her eyes, "that Bob would never go that kind of distance for me."

"Don't sell yourself short Donna. I'm sure Bob would walk over hot coals for you."

"Yeah, right. Are we talking about the same Bob?"

They merged into the North Branch of the Sandy Creek and continued downstream. Soon they paddled past the outlet into Lake Ontario and headed south down the beach to the spot where Tom and Annie sat so many years ago. Tom turned the canoe and slid the bow onto the beach. "You can step out, Donna, and pull the bow up on the beach." She did and Tom stepped out, grabbed the other side and pulled the canoe up onto the shore. Donna took off her life jacket and tossed it back in the canoe and grabbed her beach bag. Tom took the cooler and walked up the beach.

"Somewhere near here is where Annie and I were when I asked her to marry me. We went for a swim right out there. Want to go?"

Tom pulled off his pants and shirt and ran into the water. Donna said okay and stripped down to her suit and ran in behind him. "Oh my god, Tom. It's cold!"

Tom dove into a wave and came up on his back. He laughed, "Just dive in. It's not that bad!"

Donna dove in and swam out to Tom. She stopped to tread water. "That's enough for me. I'm freezing." She turned and headed back to shore.

Donna used her towel to dry off and yelled out to Tom, "I'm going over the dune to change." Tom waved and she went out of sight. He slowly headed for shore, swimming on his back until his butt hit bottom. He just sat there for awhile until Donna returned.

"Aren't you cold, Tom?"

"No, the water is warm here." He stood up, "I'll be right back," then walked over the dune to change.

When Tom returned he sat down next to Donna on the beach, shortly before the sun began to set. "I brought some refreshments, if you'd like something to drink?"

"What do you have?"

"I have light beer, diet soda, and water. What would you like?"

"I'll have the soda, please."

"And I'll have the water."

"Water? I expected you to have a beer."

"No, I stopped drinking beer after Annie took me on that first camping trip. I needed to get into shape, and eating and drinking the right things was where I started. I said, 'from now on the body is a temple.' Annie laughed, 'Yeah, right, until we get home and you order a pizza and a beer for dinner.' She was pleasantly surprised, to say the least. I try very hard to eat and drink the right things and exercise, almost daily."

"Do you think we should be heading back, Tom?"

"Well, I'd like to watch the sun set, if you don't mind. That's when I asked her to marry me."

"Do you remember how you said it and just what you said?"

"Oh yes. It's as clear in my mind as if it were yesterday. I was lying on the beach, on my right side, supporting my head with my right hand. The sun was setting, much as it is now. The sky was absolutely beautiful. Annie sat with her back against my stomach, sipping on a glass of wine. I was holding the ring in my left hand and I said, 'The sun setting marks the end of another day Annie. Let's start a new day, a new life, as husband and wife.' And I showed her the ring. 'Will you marry me, Annie Asland?' She gasped for air and placed her hand over her mouth as the tears began to flow. Annie looked at me, unable to speak and shook her head yes."

"Oh Tom, that sounds beautiful."

Tom got emotional, wiped the tears from his eyes. "It was, it really was."

Tom and Donna put everything back in the canoe. She got in the front and Tom pushed them off. "Do you know the way back in the dark, Tom?"

"Yes, we'll be alright. The sky is basically clear and the moon will be up shortly." As they headed through the outlet.

In Adams, a different mood was brewing. Young Ronnie O. Barns, known to his friends as Rock-o, a man of about twenty-six years with a slender build and shaved head, was watching a petite cashier in the local Seven-Eleven. Thoughts ran through his mind of what he'd like to do to her if he could get her alone. He had everything he needed: a hooded sweatshirt, a ski mask, duct tape and a hood for her head. And best of all, a bottle of chloroform. He continued to watch and wait for his chance.

The parking lot was empty and there were no customers in the sub shop. The slender man, Rock-o, pulled on his ski mask, put his hood up and soaked his handkerchief with the chloroform. With no customers in the store, the cashier was stocking the shelves. She didn't pay any attention when the door opened and a man walked in. She continued to work. The masked man walked directly toward her, threw one arm around her waist and covered her mouth with the chloro-form-soaked handkerchief. The clerk tried to scream but only muffled sounds came out. She fought with everything she had, digging and scratching at her attacker. He was stronger than she and her efforts were useless. Soon the gas took its effect and she slumped in his arms, defenseless.

His actions were quick and his timing perfect. She was over his shoulder and out the door in less than a minute. He had her in his car with duct tape over month, a hood over her eyes and her hands taped behind her back in less than three minutes. Then he drove out of the parking lot and headed out of town, completely unnoticed.

A local resident entered the store and walked straight to the beer cooler and removed a six-pack. He walked to the counter, placed the six-pack on it and waited. No one came to the register. "Hello." No answer. Thinking the clerk might be in the bathroom, he waited a while longer. Then another customer came in and picked up a loaf of bread. He too waited at the counter.

"Is anyone here?"

"I haven't seen anyone."

The second man walked past the ends of the rows of shelves and saw a box of can goods strewn all over. With panic in his voice. "CALL 911! Something happened here."

The village police were there in five minutes. The would-be customers were waiting outside. Patrolman Higgins exited his cruiser and asked, "What have we got?"

"We're not really sure. There is no one in the store and there's a mess in one of the aisles. We decided to wait out here in case there's someone out back, with who knows what on his mind. Or in his pocket, for that matter!"

Patrolman Higgins drew his nine millimeter Glock and cautiously entered the store, just as the State Police arrived on the scene. Higgins waited for the troopers to enter the store. Cautiously checking the storage area and all the coolers, they determined that there was no one in the store. Trooper Wright inspected the aisle with the canned goods strewn all over and discovered the handkerchief. He carefully picked it up with a pencil and took a whiff of it and put it in an evidence bag. "I think its chloroform. We're probably dealing with an abduction."

Trooper Wright asked Patrolman Higgins to get the store manager there. "Will do."

Then Trooper Wright called on his radio. "Dispatch, this is Trooper Wright at the Seven-Eleven in Adams. We request a detective at the scene. We believe we have an abduction."

"Ten-four, Trooper Wright. Detective Whallin is en route."

"Ten-four."

Store manager Trudy Price was escorted into the store by Patrolman Higgins and introduced to the troopers. "Ms. Price, who is supposed to be working tonight?"

"Bonnie Kellogg. She's twenty one, single, very attractive and reliable."

"Any chance she just ran off with a boyfriend?"

"I would say no, and I don't believe she has a boyfriend."

"Would you check the register to see if this may also be a robbery?"

Ms. Price checked the till. "It's full. There doesn't seem to be anything missing. I won't know for sure until I check tonight's receipts."

"Ms. Price, do you have a picture of Ms. Kellogg?"

"Yes I do. I make a copy of every applicant's driver's license and attach it to their application."

"Could we have that, please?"

"I'll get it for you. Here is her application, with home address, phone number, and emergency contact."

Trooper Wright gave the Patrolman the information and asked him to check her residence. "Maybe she's there. Also call her emergency contact. They may have some insight as to her whereabouts."

Detective Whallin arrived at the scene in his usual western appearance. "What do we have, Trooper?"

"Detective, it appears we have an abduction. The cashier is missing and the register doesn't appear to have been touched. And I discovered a handkerchief on the floor near a disturbance in one of the aisles. I believe it's soaked in chloroform."

"Anything else trooper?"

"The cashier is young and attractive, very reliable and doesn't appear to have a boyfriend detective."

"Did anyone see anything or anyone suspicious?"

"I haven't had anyone come forward yet. I was just about to check the sub shop next door when you arrived, sir."

"Ok, attend to that, Trooper."

"Yes sir."

Whallin called his headquarters. "Dispatch, this is Detective Whallin, requesting a BOLO on a Bonnie Kellogg, female, twenty- one years. Attractive blond, five feet two inches, a hundred and ten pounds. Anyone with information call etc. etc."

"Ten-four."

Patrolman Higgins radioed in. "Ms. Kellogg is not at her residence, and emergency contact has no information on her location."

Trooper Wright entered the sub shop and asked the staff if anyone had seen anything suspicious that evening. A young lady, about seventeen spoke up.

"I may have."

"What did you see?"

I saw a man sitting in a black or a dark colored car most of the evening. He would sit for awhile then move his car and sit and then move it again. He never got out, just kept moving it."

"Did you see the driver?"

"Not to know who he was, just that he was a white male with a shaved head. I mentioned it to Ron."

Ron stepped forward. "Yes she did. I kind of kept an eye on him. Then he was gone and we didn't see him again."

"You didn't get a plate number, by any chance?"

"No, sorry."

"Okay. Thanks for your help."

Trooper Wright went back to the Seven-Eleven and relayed the information to Detective Whallin.

"Dispatch, this is Detective Whallin, requesting an all-points on a black late model sedan, driven by a white male with a shaved head. No plate or model. Believe to have kidnapped one Bonnie Kellogg: white female, twenty-one years old, last seen wearing a South Jeff sweat shirt and jeans."

"Ten-Four."

Tom and Donna paddled their canoe up the North Branch of the Sandy Creek. The moon came out, making it easy to find the outlet to Lakeview Pond. They paddled on through the dark and eventually entered the pond. About two hours after leaving the beach they slid their canoe up onto the boat launch. Donna jumped out and pulled the bow up higher. Tom stepped out and asked, "Well, how you feel Donna?"

"I think my arms are going to fall off and my back is killing me." Tom laughed. "Give me your paddle, Tom. I'll put them it the truck. And just leave the cooler and my beach bag. I'll get them on the next trip."

Tom rolled the canoe over and walked it up until the yoke slipped over his head and rested on his shoulders. Then with the canoe balanced the bow came off the ground and he carried it to the truck. He stuck the bow up over the cab then slid the stern up onto the rack. Donna returned with the beach bag and cooler.

"Do you need help tying it down Tom?"

"No, I can get it okay."

"That's good, because I need to make a nature call." Donna walked to the end of the parking lot and into the bushes.

As Tom was tying the canoe down, another car pulled into the parking area, stopping about fifty yards from Tom's truck. The driver got out of the front seat of a dark sedan and obviously didn't see Tom parked there. He opened the rear door and pulled something from the back seat. Tom paid little attention until he heard what sounded like a muffled scream. He stopped what he was doing and watched as the man started tearing at the clothes of his victim, who seemed to be a young woman. She continued to scream as she kicked at him and tried to fight him off.

Tom knew she was in trouble and hollered, "HEY! WHAT'S GOING ON?" He headed toward the car.

Rock-o, surprised by the question and not expecting anyone to be there, responded by pulling a hand gun from his waist band, pointing it in the direction from which the voice came and yelling, "NONE OF YOUR GODDAMN BUSINESS!" He fired the pistol. Tom ducked, turned around and was running back toward the truck when he saw the muzzle flash and heard the small-caliber pop. Rock-o fired again and again, walking toward Tom's truck. Tom ran around the truck and into the brush, where he hid without making a sound.

With Rock-o pursuing Tom, Bonnie wasted no time in dragging her head across the ground until she managed to get the hood off. Though it was dark, she could see well enough to get to her feet and run off in the opposite direction. She too ran into the brush and out of sight. Rock-o returned to his car to find his prize gone and, knowing it wouldn't be long before police arrived, he shouted, "DAMN IT," picked up the discarded hood, threw it in the back and kicked the rear door closed. Before he got into the front seat he threw the small caliber hand gun out into the pond. He got into his car and slammed the door. With the engine running, he dropped it into gear, spun 180 degrees and sped out, heading for the main road.

Tom wanted to get all the information he could. As the slender man headed for his car, Tom moved through the tall grass at the edge of the road and stayed out of sight. He saw that the shooter was a white man with a shaved head. He was rail-thin and drove a dark-colored older model Ford sedan. As the man drove by, Tom saw and memorized a rear plate number -- WR 2621. He watched him turn right when he hit the main road.

Tom walked out of the tall grass and headed for his truck. As he got close he could hear Donna crying. He broke into a trot and yelled, "Donna, are you all right?" When he walked around the front of the truck he saw Donna on her knees, crying uncontrollably. "Are you hurt?" She didn't respond, just kept crying. Tom slowly moved closer and looked over her shoulder.

The image he saw threw him backwards. It landed him on his ass. Shocked, he gasped for air, his eyes bulging in their sockets. He kicked his way backwards not believing what he saw. Donna was holding *him*. *"I'M DEAD!"*

Tom, almost hysterical, looked again. *"THAT'S ME! I'M DEAD! I'M REALLY DEAD. OH MY GOD, WHAT HAPPENED? HOW DID THIS HAPPEN?"* Donna was sitting on the ground, holding his head, not knowing what to do. Tom stood up, still in shock, turned around and caught a glimpse of himself in the truck's side-view mirror. He did a double take. *"I look like I'm about twenty-three again. I'm twenty three and dead."*

Bonnie Kellogg saw the car drive off. She got back onto her feet and walked out of the brush. She could hear someone crying. Bonnie walked to the back of Tom's truck. Not knowing what she would see, she slowly looked around to the other side. There was a woman, crying over someone lying on the ground. Unable to speak, she nudged Donna with her foot. Donna gave a short gasp, turned around and saw the young woman with tape over her mouth. She stood and gently removed the tape. The first words out of the girl's mouth were, "Is he alright?"

Donna, choking to speak, "No, I'm sure he's dead. He has no pulse."

"That man saved my life. If he hadn't distracted that creep, I never would have gotten away."

Still choking back tears. "Here, let me get your hands free."

Donna got the tape off Bonnie's wrists.

"My name is Bonnie."

Sniffling, "I'm Donna."

"Do you have a cell phone Donna?"

Donna shook her head. "Yes, I do. It's on the front seat of the truck."

"I'll get it Donna. We should call the police."

"Yes, you're right. I wasn't thinking."

Bonnie pushed 911 and then send.

"911, what is your emergency?"

"My name is Bonnie Kellogg. I was kidnapped from the Seven-Eleven store in Adams. I am somewhere near a pond."

Talking through a runny nose and sniffling. "We are at Lakeview Pond, at the end of Pierrepont Place, west of Route 3."

Bonnie repeated the message. "We need an ambulance. A man has been shot!"

"Is he breathing?"

"No. He doesn't have a pulse either."

"Is the person who shot him still there?"

"No, he drove away."

"Who else is there with you?"

"Just one other woman, her name is Donna. I assume to be his wife."

"I'm not his wife. I'm just his neighbor."

"I have dispatched an ambulance and the State Police to your location. They should be arriving in about ten minutes. Please stay on the line."

Trooper Wright stepped back into the Seven-Eleven.

"Detective?"

"Yes, Trooper?"

"There's an ambulance responding to Lakeview Pond. Bonnie Kellogg made the call. Someone has been shot!"

Detective Whallin asked Patrolman Higgins to secure the Seven-Eleven crime scene and wait for investigators. The troopers and Detective Whallin went, lights flashing and sirens wailing, to Lakeview Pond.

The ambulance had to wait at Route 3 until police made sure it was safe for first responders to enter the scene. With weapons drawn, the troopers cleared the scene and ordered the ambulance forward. Detective Whallin also drove in.

The first responders asked if anyone needed medical attention. Donna sitting on the tail gate of the truck. "I'm fine. But Tom is over here, behind the truck. I'm sure he's dead."

Bonnie Kellogg leaning against the side of the truck. "I'm okay, but I'd like a blanket to cover up with. My clothes are a little ripped. And don't touch my fingers. I scratched him good. Hopefully I have some DNA under my nails."

Detective Whallin heard that statement. "Good for you! I'm Detective Whallin of the New York State Police. Do you know who your abductor was, Ms. Kellogg?"

"No, I don't."

"Can you describe him?"

"All I saw were his white hands. He gassed me with something in the store. After that I had a hood over my head, my hands tied behind my back and tape over my mouth. I'm sorry I can't help you with more."

"If you got us some DNA you did great, young lady. Trooper Wright, take Ms. Kellogg to the ambulance. I want you to collect the evidence from under her nails, bag and tag."

"Yes sir."

He walked over to the other lady and recognized Donna Thompson from their earlier conversations about Tom Blake and the mysterious woman that Donna had seen around Tom's home.

"Hello again, Detective."

"Hello. Aren't you Mrs. Thompson? Do you know the deceased?"

"Yes, he's my neighbor, Thomas Blake."

"The same Thomas Blake who just lost his wife?"

"Yes, Detective, he's the same Tom Blake."

"Well, Mrs. Thompson, what can you tell me? Did you see the gunman? And do you think this has any connection with your previous suspicions?"

"No, I didn't see the gunman. And I'm sure there is no connection with the young woman that I saw before. The girl who was abducted was definitely not the woman I saw at Tom's house."

Chocking back the tears. "Tom and I came back from canoeing. I had to make a nature call. He was tying the canoe on the truck while I was in the bushes. I heard the yelling and then some pops, like fire crackers, then a car speeding away. When I came out of the brush, I found Tom lying there on the ground. He wasn't moving. I thought he was unconscious, until I saw the blood. I shook him and tried to get him to respond to me, but he wouldn't, he just laid there. When I felt for a pulse there was nothing."

"You didn't see the gunman, his car, anything?"

"No I didn't, Detective. I'm sorry. I was way over there in the brush. I'm sorry!"

"That's okay, Mrs. Thompson. Let the first responders check you over, then I'll have one of the troopers take you home. Do you still have my card? If you think of, or remember anything?"

"Yes, I have it at home."

"Good. And please, give me a call if there's anything at all."

"Of course I will, Detective."

Donna waited while the first responders checked Bonnie over. While she waited she dialed Bob's cell number. "Hello."

"Bob?"

"Yes, who is this?"

"It's me, Donna."

"Donna, what's wrong? You sound hysterical."

"It's Tom. He's been murdered!"

"WHAT? Who... what... oh my god. Are YOU all right?"

"Yes, I'll be fine. But Bob ... I need you!"

"I'm coming home right away. I'll be on the first flight I can get. All right? I'll be there as quickly as I can. I love you, Donna."

"I love you too, Bob."

Detective Whallin called the troopers over to his cruiser. "I want this crime scene taped off. Nobody comes in until the investigators have finished their jobs, got it?"

"Yes, sir!"

The coroner arrived and took charge of the body. He confirmed the cause of death to be a small-caliber gunshot wound to the back of the head. The approximate time of death could be no more than an hour ago. "I can tell you more, Detective, after my autopsy is finished."

"Okay, thank you, doctor."

The body was then loaded into the ambulance and transported to Watertown.

A sheriff's deputy was called to take Bonnie and Donna home. Detective Whallin escorted both ladies to the squad car. "Is there someone who can stay with you ladies tonight?"

Bonnie told the detective that she had a roommate and would be fine.

"Are you sure Bonnie, I can have an officer stay with you, it's not a problem!"

"Thank you, I'll be fine. I live in the village."

"Mrs. Thompson?"

"My husband was in Florida on business and will soon be on his way home.

"All right, deputy. I want you to stay in Mrs. Thompson's driveway until her husband gets home. She is not to be alone. If she wants you inside her house, that's all the better. Okay, deputy?"

"Yes sir."

"I would like an official statement from both of you ladies sometime tomorrow morning, in my office." Bonnie and Donna both agreed. Detective Whallin opened the deputies car door for Bonnie and Donna to get in. "Be safe ladies, don't hesitate to call." He closed their door.

During the drive to Adams, Donna and Bonnie just hugged each other. It had been a frightening experience for both of them. The deputy pulled up in front of Bonnie's residence and put his cruiser in park. "Before I take you to your door, I just want to say that both of you have been through a traumatizing experience. Don't be afraid to seek out someone professional to talk to. It's better if you don't try to deal with this on your own."

In unascend. "Thank you, Deputy."

He got out and opened Bonnie's door and walked her to her door. Her roommate answered their knock. The sheriff's deputy instructed her roommate that Bonnie was not, under any circumstances, to be left alone. "Keep all your doors and windows locked. Have your cell phone handy and don't be afraid to call 911. This guy is still out there. And Bonnie needs to report to Detective Whallin's office sometime tomorrow morning."

"Yes sir, we understand." Both girls nodded.

Returning to his cruiser, the deputy then took Donna home to Horner Drive. He opened her door and walked her up the steps.

"If you don't mind, deputy, I'd like you to come in, at least for coffee."

"Yes ma'am, coffee sounds really good about now."

Donna unlocked the front door. They entered and locked it behind them. "Come on in to the kitchen, deputy. I'm sorry, what is your name? I don't want to call you deputy all night."

"Ted. My name is Ted, ma'am."

Donna made a pot of coffee and poured a cup for Ted. "Do you take cream or sugar, Ted?"

"No thanks, black is fine."

"Bring your coffee into the living room. It's a little more comfortable there." Donna sat with her knees up and feet in the chair, and Ted sat on the couch. They made idle chitchat until Donna fell asleep. Ted covered her with the afghan from the back of the couch and turned all the lights off but one.

Morning came. Donna opened her eyes and stretched in the chair. Ted was still sitting on the couch, wide awake. "Good morning, ma'am."

"Oh, good morning, Ted. Did you get any sleep?"

"No, I managed to stay awake. I did drink all of your coffee, though."

Rubbing her eyes, "I'll make a fresh pot." She fixed the coffee pot and turned it on. "If you don't mind Ted, I'd like to take a shower and freshen up." Ted, not knowing exactly how to respond, shrugged his shoulders and nodded his head.

At about nine a.m. Bob pulled into the driveway, got out of his car and ran to the house. Ted met him at the door. Bob, stunned to see a sheriff in his house asked, "Who are you? Is my wife alright?"

"I'm a deputy sheriff, assigned to stay with Mrs. Thompson until her husband gets home."

"Well, I'm her husband."

Ted yelled, "MRS. THOMPSON, IS THIS YOUR HUS-BAND?"

Donna came out of the bedroom and walked up the hall with her arms outstretched, put them around Bob's neck and gave him a big hug. "Oh Bob, it was awful."

Ted said, "I'll take that as a yes."

Donna wiped the tears from her eyes, smiled at Ted. "I'm sorry, Ted. Yes, this is my husband Bob." The two men shook hands.

"If you are okay then, Mrs. Thompson, I'll be leaving."

"Yes Ted, I'll be fine now. Thank you for staying with me."

"It was no trouble. And don't forget to make your statement at Detective Whallin's office this morning."

"Yes, I won't forget. My husband and I will be there." Bob chimed in, "Thank you, deputy."

"No problem, sir."

The front door closed and Bob put his arms around Donna.

"Tom is dead? What on earth happened?"

"Come to the kitchen and get yourself a cup of coffee. I'll tell you everything."

Bob poured two cups and sat down. "Tom came over to the house on Wednesday looking for you......"

After Donna finished telling Bob the whole story she looked at the clock. "We have to go. I have to make my statement at the State Police barracks this morning." They locked the house and drove through Watertown to the barracks on Route 37.

Bob and Donna entered the building and walked to the front desk. Sergeant Williams asked, "May I help you?"

"Yes, I'm Donna Thompson. I'm here to make my statement to Detective Whallin."

"Have a seat, Mrs. Thompson. Detective Whallin is interviewing Ms. Kellogg. I'm sure it won't take long."

"Thank you Sergeant."

Sergeant Williams smiled, Bob and Donna took a seat.

About thirty minutes passed and Bonnie Kellogg came out of Detective Whallin's office. She walked straight to Donna. Donna stood and they hugged each other.

"How you doing Donna?"

"It's been a real shock. How about you?"

"I didn't sleep much. I just kept reliving it all night, over and over. I don't think I'll be able to go back to work until they catch him, you know?"

"Do you think he'll come after either of us Bonnie?"

"I don't know. What I do know is that I won't ever be alone until they do. Well, I've got to go. Be safe."

"You too, Bonnie."

Whallin came out of his office. "Mr. and Mrs. Thompson, come in please." They entered the office and Donna introduced her husband to Detective Whallin. "Have a seat please.

Mrs. Thompson, I'm going to record our conversation on two devices to be sure we get it. This is a precaution in case one device fails during the interview, okay?"

"That's fine Detective."

"Please state your name, address, phone number, the date, and case number, seventeen thirty three, Blake murder".

"My name is Donna Thompson. I reside at ............." She started at the beginning, when Tom had come to the house looking for her husband Bob. She didn't leave anything out, up to the point when she found Tom on the ground. That's when she lost it. She began crying and apologizing for her emotion.

"That's okay, I understand Mrs. Thompson." Bob sat next to Donna and held her shoulder.

"That's all for now, Mrs. Thompson. If you think of anything else, don't hesitate to call. Also, please be careful. It's not wise to be alone. He's still out there."

Bob spoke. "Can I ask, Detective, what information do you have?"

"At this point, we don't have much. He is a slender-built white male with a shaved head, driving a dark-colored car. The best lead that we have is possible DNA from under Ms. Kellogg's fingernails. And it takes about two weeks to get the results back from that. We hope there'll be a match in the data base. If not, it's not much help until we have a suspect."

"Thank you, Detective."

"Thank you for coming in."

They left the barracks and headed for home. Bob said, "I have some time coming. I'll take a few days and stay at home."

"Take a few days! OH MY GOD BOB, I FORGOT TO CALL THE SCHOOL." Donna pulled out her cell phone and quickly called the office.

"South Jeff Elementary School, Adams Center, may I help you?"

"Yes, this is Donna Thompson."

"Yes. Oh my god, Donna, are you alright? It's all over the news!"

"Yes, I'm fine, a little shaken up. Other than that, I'll be fine. I'm sorry I didn't call sooner."

"That's not a problem. We really didn't expect you in. We have your back."

"Listen, I really don't have any idea how this will proceed. Can I just take a few days?"

"Yes, oh yes. The superintendent said if you called in, to let you know that it's okay to take all the time you need."

"Oh, that's a relief. Thank you so much. I'll be back as quick as I can. Bye for now."

"Okay, bye-bye."

The phone rang in Detective Whallin's office. "Detective Whallin."

"Detective, this is the county coroner."

"Yes doctor. What do you have?"

"I have confirmed that the cause of death was a gunshot wound to the back of the head. I retrieved a small caliber projectile, possibly a .22. I sent that over to ballistics for analysis."

"Was there any stippling, Doctor?"

"No, there was not. The shot was taken from a distance, not point blank. Death was instantaneous. I don't believe he knew what hit him. Tox screen shows that there were no drugs or alcohol in his system. His physical condition was that of a much younger man. I would say he worked out almost every day. I am about finished. The body should be released no later than tomorrow at four o'clock. Oh, by the way, Detective, do you have a next of kin?"

"Good question, Doctor. I'll let you know."


Bob and Donna were headed for home. "It's about lunch time, dear. Would you like to stop for a bite to eat?"

"Yes, now that you mention it, I am hungry. But Bob, I really don't want to stop anywhere. Everyone will be looking, staring and talking about me. Can we just get something at home, please?"

"Yes, sure, whatever you want."

"I can order a pizza to be delivered Bob. I have my phone."

"That works for me."

Donna dialed the number and ordered a Supreme, to be delivered.

"That will be twelve dollars in about forty-five minutes."

"Thank you." Donna hung up the phone.

They arrived home. While walking up the walk, Donna stopped in her tracks and turned to Bob. Her eyes were wide.

"Donna, what is it?"

"We may have made a big mistake!" Donna turned and ran to the house. Bob was right behind her. She quickly unlocked the door, stepped in and locked it behind her.

"What is it, Donna? What's wrong?"

"The pizza delivery guy. When he comes, you answer the door and make sure he doesn't have a shaved head!" Donna started pacing the floor nervously. "Bob, I'm scared. I'm a witness. HE WANTS ME DEAD, BOB! We have to be careful." Donna was shaking her hands as she paced.

"Okay, it's okay," Bob assured her. "I'll answer the door."

"Oh, Bob," Donna was walking back and forth. "I've never felt like this before. Hold me, please."

Bob put his arms around Donna and held her tight. "It's all right, I've got you. Calm down, calm down. Donna, you've been traumatized! I'm going to call our doctor and get something to calm you down." Bob grabbed his phone and quickly dialed the number.

"Doctor Kent's office."

"Yes, this is Robert Thompson. May I speak to the doctor, please?"

"One moment, sir. The doctor has been expecting your call."

"Mr. Thompson, this is Doctor Kent. How is your wife?"

"She is extremely anxious, doctor. Can you give her something to calm her down?"

"Yes, of course. I heard about it on the news. I was afraid this might happen, given the circumstances. I have something here that should help. I'll have my receptionist bring it down. I'm sure she doesn't want to go out and you don't want to leave her alone."

"No, that's right, Doctor. Thank you very much."

"She should only take one every four hours to help her relax. If she takes more than that she may start to hallucinate. My secretary's name is Sandy Brown and she will be driving a red Ford Mustang."

"Thank you again, Doctor."

"Don't be afraid to call if you need anything else, Mr. Thompson, and good luck. I'm sure you have your hands full."

Bob hung up just as the door bell rang. Donna quickly went into the kitchen. Bob opened the curtain and looked at the delivery boy and smiled. He opened the front door, handed the young man fifteen dollars, said, "Thank you" and closed the door. He stood for just a minute, and opened the door again. The young man said, "Did you forget something, sir?"

Bob smiled sheepishly, took the pizza from his hands and thanked him again.

Donna got out plates and a couple of sodas. Bob came into the kitchen smiling. Donna looked a little wide-eyed. "It's alright. He had hair down to his shoulders."

They were both eating slices of pizza when the doorbell rang again. Bob looked out the window and saw the red mustang. He opened the door and saw an attractive little redhead.

"Mr. Thompson, I'm Sandy Brown. This is from Dr. Kent, for your wife."

"Thank you so much. It was so kind of Dr. Kent to send the pills over."

"You're welcome, sir," Sandy added before he closed the door.

Donna wasted no time in taking her first pill. "I hope this works Bob, I don't like feeling so anxious." They each ate one more slice of pizza. Then Donna went to their bedroom and fell asleep. *"It's probably the best thing for her,"* Bob thought.

Fifteen minutes later Bob went to the bedroom to check on Donna. She was sound asleep. He covered her with a blanket and walked back to the living room, leaving the bedroom door wide open. *"I don't want her to feel alone when she wakes up."*

Donna slept soundly for three and a half hours. She awoke, pushed back the blanket and sat on the edge of the bed, rubbing her eyes. She heard Bob call her from the living room.

"Yes, Bob, what is it?" Donna asked from the bedroom. Bob got up from his chair and walked down the hall. She looked at him from the edge of the bed. "What did you want?"

"I didn't want anything."

"Well, why did you call me?"

"I didn't call you, dear. You must have been dreaming."

"Maybe." She got up and stumbled into the bathroom.

"Bob?"

"Yes, hon?"

"I'm going to take a quick shower. Would you put on a pot of coffee?"

"Sure thing."

"Thank you."

Donna stepped into a steaming hot shower, washed her face and hair. It felt so good she hated to stop. She finally dried off, then stood in front of the sink and brushed her teeth. With clean clothes on she felt like a new woman. She slid into her slippers and walked into the kitchen. The bottle of pills that Dr. Kent had given her was on the window sill over the sink. She didn't hesitate. She opened the bottle and took one. *"I really don't want that feeling of hysteria to return."*

Donna poured herself a cup of coffee, leaned against the sink and sipped. Again she thought she heard Bob call her. "Yes Bob, what is it?"

Bob left the living room and went to the kitchen. "Did you call me?"

"I thought you called *me*."

"No, maybe you heard the television."

"I guess so, sorry."

"No problem, honey."

Donna finished her coffee, walked to the living room doorway. "What would you like for dinner, Bob?"

He got up. "I'll fix dinner. What would you like, hon?"

"I'm not really hungry. Maybe just soup and a sandwich."

"Yeah, that sounds good. I'll have it ready in just a moment."

"Thanks, Bob. It's really nice of you."

"I don't mind at all."

Donna sat in her chair in the living room and again closed her eyes. She laid her head against the back of the chair and dozed off. She heard Bob call her again. She got up and walked back into the kitchen.

"Yes, Bob, what is it?"

He had a quizzical look on his face. "I didn't say anything."

"You didn't just call me?"

"No honey I didn't"

"Well, when you do, speak a little clearer, would you. You're mumbling." Donna returned to her favorite chair and again fell right to sleep.

A short while later, Bob put dinner on the table, went into the living room and shook Donna gently. She opened her eyes and looked up at Bob.

"Dinner's ready hon."

Together they went to the table. Donna looked at the light meal. "M-m-m-m, tomato soup and grilled cheese. You know Bob, my dad used to fix this for us kids every Saturday. We would eat an entire loaf of bread."

Bob smiled. "Are you feeling better?"

"Yes, now that you mention it, I do feel pretty good. I think the sleep was the best thing for me."

"Well, I can't imagine what you went through."

"I was terrified, just absolutely terrified. I think the pills help."

"I'm sure they help. Just don't overdo ok?"

"Well, I've got you to keep an eye on me. And frankly, Bob, I really don't want to be alone right now."

After dinner they retired to the living room to watch a little television. Bob made it a point to avoid the news. At around 7:15 the phone rang. "Hello."

"Mr. Thompson?"

"Yes."

"This is Detective Whallin."

"Yes, Detective. How can I help you?"

"The coroner has completed the autopsy on Mr. Blake and his body is ready to be released to the next of kin. Do you have any idea who that might be?"

"That's a good question. Tom and his wife didn't have any children. Nor did they have any siblings. His mother is the only surviving parent and she is in a nursing home. What I can tell you is that the Raymond Weldon Funeral Home in Adams arranged the services for his wife. I'm sure Tom would want them to handle his service as well."

"Thank you, Mr. Thompson. I'll give them a call."

At ten o'clock Donna was ready for bed. She went to the kitchen for a drink of water and took another pill. "Good night, Bob. I'm going to bed now."

"Good night, hon. I'll be there in just a moment."

"Take your time. Finish watching your show." Donna slipped into bed and fell right to sleep.

The next morning Donna got up and went to the kitchen to make coffee, leaving Bob asleep in bed. She went to the sink for a drink and took another pill. The house was completely quiet. Yet standing in the kitchen, she thought she could hear Bob calling her. She stepped to the living room door and listened. She was sure that he was calling her. Donna walked to the bedroom door and looked in to see Bob sound asleep.

Back in the kitchen she stood by the sink and closed her eyes and listened. She knew that she was hearing something, but what? *"I think I'm hearing my name, but that's all. I can't make out anything else. It's just a murmur."*

The coffee was ready and Donna poured herself a cup. Leaning against the sink, sipping, she listened intently. Bob walked into the kitchen. "Good morning, hon."

"Morning."

"Bob?"

"Yeah?"

"Fix your coffee. I want you to do something for me."

"Sure." He fixed his coffee, stood by Donna. "What's up?"

"Bob, do you hear anything?"

"Like what?"

"Like ..... ," She stopped talking and looked straight at Bob. "DO NOT PATRONIZE ME, BOB. I'M SERIOUS. I MEAN IT!

"Okay, okay. What do YOU hear?"

"No, I want you to tell me what *YOU* hear. Put your back against the sink, sip your coffee and listen."

Bob did just as she asked. Put his back against the sink and sipped his coffee. Donna stood right beside him, hearing the murmur.

"Do you hear anything, Bob?"

"No, not yet."

"Try closing your eyes and concentrate."

Bob closed his eyes. He didn't even move. Standing right beside him, Donna heard the voice.

"Okay Bob, tell me you didn't hear that!"

"I'm sorry, hon. I do not hear a thing!"

"I must be going out of my mind."

"How many pills have you taken hon?"

"Just the one every four hours, why?"

"Doctor Kent said no more than that, because you could hallucinate."

"Bob, I don't think I'm hallucinating. Do you want to know what I think? I think my best friend, my very best friend in the whole world, is trying to talk to me. That's what I think. There I said it. Now call me crazy."

Bob wrinkled up his face, tipped his head and said in a soft voice, "Annie? You think Annie is trying to talk to you?"

Donna started to pace back and forth. "Yes, I do, I really do, and I can't make out what she is trying to say. Help me Bob, please!"

Bob gave her a big hug. She stepped back and Bob rubbed his head. "I'd help if I could, but I don't know how!"

Donna kept pacing, then started shaking her hands. "Think, Donna, think," she kept saying. Then she stopped, her eyes opened. "The internet! I'll look on the internet."

She put her laptop on the counter, hit Internet Explorer, typed in "psychic" and hit search. A whole list of psychics came up. "Oh my god, Bob. There are a million of them."

"What are you trying to do?"

"I want to ask for help. Which one do I ask?"

"Just pick one, I guess hon."

"'Wanda', she sounds like a gypsy." Donna clicked on "Wanda." Instantly a response came back.

*This is Wanda, are you looking for a love connection?*

"No, I'm not. I'm looking for a little help. Can you help me?"

*"It depends, child. What kind of help are you seeking?"*

"I think my best friend is trying to contact me from the other side and I can't make out what she is saying. Can you help me?"

*"I'll try, child. I want you to sit in the spot where the voice is coming through. Sit in a chair with your hands in your lap and close your eyes and concentrate on your friend's name. The room must be quiet. There must not be any distraction."*

"I'll try."

Donna grabbed a chair and placed it by the kitchen sink. She sat down and put her hands in her lap, closed her eyes and thought only of Annie. Soon she could hear the murmur. She squeezed her eyes tighter and tighter, still unable to understand what Annie was saying. Thirty minutes passed before Donna got up and went back to the computer.

"Anything Donna?"

"No Bob, I still can't make out what she is saying."

"Wanda?" she typed.

*"Yes, this is Wanda. How can I help?"*

"It's not working. I can't make out what she is saying."

*"Do you have anything that belonged to your friend, something that she cherished?"*

"Yes, yes I do."

*"Get it and hold it in your hands and try again."*

"Okay, I will."

Donna ran into the living room and grabbed Annie's coffee cup. *Annie Blake, Teacher of the Year, 2005.* Donna ran back to the kitchen and sat in her chair, holding the cup. She closed her eyes and concentrated again on Annie and only Annie. She closed her eyes tighter and tighter, heard the murmur. She tried and tried, still not quite able to make it out. Another thirty minutes passed. Bob stood quietly by her side, not making a sound, watching his wife.

Finally Donna went back to the computer. "Wanda?" she typed.

*"This is Wanda, how can I help."*

She typed "It's not working! I did just what you ask and I can't understand what she is saying to me."

*"If you cannot understand her then you are trying to contact the wrong person child. Your best friend is not the one trying to reach you. It's someone else!"*

Donna, wide-eyed, looked at Bob. "If it's not Annie, then who can it be?"

Bob, rubbing his hair and shaking his head. "I don't know, hon. I really don't know."

Donna, pacing back and forth trying to think, stopped and looked directly at Bob. "Tom! Could it be Tom? IT IS, IT HAS TO BE HIM!"

Donna ran to her purse and dumped everything on the table. Bob calmly asked, "What are you looking for?"

"The keys. Tom gave me the keys to his house. I need to find something he holds dear to him, something very special." Donna picked up the keys and headed for the door.

Bob yelled, "Wait for me! I don't want you to be alone." He ran after her.

Donna ran across the lawn and up the front steps, stuck the key in the lock and turned the knob. The door opened and they walked in.

"What are we looking for hon?"

"We need something special, an article that means a lot to him."

Bob went to the kitchen and saw Annie's picture and urn. Maybe! He went to Tom's shop; nothing there but tools. He went back upstairs. "The only thing I found is Annie's urn and this picture of her."

"That might work Bob, but let's keep looking."

Donna went into the bedroom and saw the manila envelope on the wall. She walked over to it and read "*THIS IS MY FINAL REQUEST*." "I'VE GOT IT BOB!" Donna took it down and ran back out the door. Bob locked and closed the door behind him.

Donna ran back into her kitchen and sat in the chair. She was out of breath, fanning her face with the envelope until Bob came in. "Calm down Donna, Calm down."

Donna took a few deep breaths, closed her eyes and concentrated on Tom, listening for his voice, trying to discern his words. Then she heard it!

"*DONNA!*" She gasped and sat straight up in the chair her eyes bulging and intense stare.

"Yes, yes. Tom, is it you?"

Bob jumped back against the wall, his jaw on his chest and his eyes went wide.

"*Yes, Donna, it's me. I need your help!*"

"What can I do?"

Bob could only hear what Donna was saying. But he knew she was actually talking to Tom.

"*I know who he is.*"

"You know who *who* is, Tom?"

"*The man who killed me.*"

"What do you want me to do?"

*"I want you to go back to the detective and tell him you have information on the suspect, information that will lead him to an arrest and conviction."*

"What information do you have, Tom?"

*"I know the make of his car, the license plate, his address. Donna, I even have the gun."*

She gasped again and tears filled her eyes as she stared straight ahead. "Okay, Tom. I'll call him right now."

Donna went straight to the phone and dialed the number of the State Police barracks.

"New York State Police, Sergeant Williams speaking. May I help you?"

"Hello, Sergeant. This is Donna Thompson. I'd like to speak to Detective Whallin, please."

"One moment, Ms. Thompson," the sergeant advised. Hearing the urgency in her voice, he put Donna straight through to Whallin.

"Detective Whallin speaking."

"This is Donna Thompson, Detective. Can I come to see you? I have information on our suspect for you."

"Yes, Mrs. Thompson. Of course you can come right in."

"We'll be there in thirty minutes, Detective."

"I'll be looking for you."

Bob and Donna hurried to the car and drove straight to the station. When they walked in, Sergeant Williams said, "The detective is waiting for you in the interrogation room."

They entered the interrogation room and the detective pointed to the two chairs on the opposite side of the table. "Sit down, please." They sat and Donna held the manila envelope in her lap.

"You have information for me, Mrs. Thompson?"

"Yes, I believe that I do."

"Yesterday you had nothing. How is it that today, you suddenly have some information?"

"I'm not really sure. I guess you could say it just came to me."

"It *came* to you? Let me ask you this, Mrs. Thompson. Your eyes are really dilated. Are you taking any medication?"

"Dr. Kent gave me something to help me relax. Other than that, no."

"I see. So this information you have just *came* to you." Whallin was not sure what to make of Donna Thompson's new insight.

"Yes, Detective, it did."

"I mean no offense, Mrs. Thompson, but I'm very busy here." The detective stood up.

Bob Thompson also stood. "You really should listen to her. Based on what I saw, you really should listen to her."

"I'm sorry, Mr. Thompson ....."

"Just give her five minutes, please. Just five minutes," Bob pleaded.

Whallin sat back down with a sigh. "Okay, Mrs. Thompson. You have five minutes."

"I won't waste your time, Detective. I'll cut right to the chase. First of all, I am not psychic, but Tom Blake contacted me."

"OKAY, THAT'S IT. WE'RE DONE!"

"Five minutes, detective, you promised her five minutes."

Again Whallin sat down, Donna continued. "I heard Tom's voice. He told me he knew who had done it. I ask, 'Who did what Tom?' *'I know who killed me, I know his name, the make of his car, the license plate number and his address. I even know where the gun is."*

Detective Whallin just sat there and shook his head. "I'm sorry Mrs. Thompson, but I find it difficult to believe a word you're saying."

Donna sensed Tom leaning over her shoulder, she closed her eyes, held the manila envelope tight to her chest and concentrated on his voice. *"Ask him to ask you a question about himself. Anything, any question. Anything at all Donna."*

"How much time do we have left, Detective?" Donna asked.

"Three minutes."

"Okay then, ask me a question about yourself; a question only you know the answer to."

"Okay, I'll play the game with you. Where was I born?"

Donna sat straight up in her chair, closed her eyes and bowed her head. With no hesitation Donna opened her eyes, looking straight at Detective Whallin, "Massachusetts, Boston to be exact."

"Where did I go to college?"

"Syracuse University. You studied pre-med but decided that wasn't for you, so you switched to criminal justice."

"You could have looked all that up. Last question, Mrs. Thompson. What do I have in the top right-hand drawer of my desk that is never, I mean *never* unlocked?"

"You have your father's shield. Number 1 – 7 – 2 – 0."

The detective's jaw dropped. He stared at Donna Thompson.

"SERGEANT WILLIAMS!"

"Yes, Detective?"

"Get me a recorder. This woman is for real. Now, Mrs. Thompson, you have my undivided attention. Please go ahead. Give me this information that "just came to you."

Donna told Whallin the facts that Tom had given her as she sat in her kitchen: *"His name is Ronnie O. Barns, AKA Rock-o. He drives an older-model Black Ford, license plate WR 2621. He resides at 117 Clinton Street in Pulaski, New York. After he shot Tom he threw the gun, a .22 caliber revolver, into the pond right in front of where his car was parked. When he got back to his car his victim,*

Bonnie Kellogg, was gone. *He was so mad he kicked the driver's side rear door shut and put a dent in it. In the back seat of his car you will find the hood that was over Ms. Kellogg's head."* Donna continued, "If you can get a DNA sample from him I'm sure it will match the sample you collected from Ms. Kellogg's fingernails. Also a DNA sample from Ms. Kellogg will match the DNA found inside the black hood that was over her head. With that, Detective, you should have enough evidence to get your conviction."

"If all of this checks out, Mrs. Thompson, we will get a conviction. As I said, *if!*"

Donna and Bob got up and headed for the door. Donna stopped, turned around. "Detective."

"Yes, Mrs. Thompson?"

"Don't bother thanking us, Tom and me. Just nail the bastard." Bob put his arm around Donna's shoulder as they walked out.

Whallin called to Williams, "Sergeant!"

"Yes, sir."

"Get a dive team to Lakeview Pond. I want that gun!"

"Right away, sir."

"And a warrant for Ronnie O. Barns, wanted for questioning in the Thomas Blake murder. And a search warrant for his car, a late model dark Ford. License plate: WR 2621. Let's bring him in for a chat before he decides to leave the state."

Sergeant Williams nodded his head vigorously and closed the door.

Shortly after Detective Whallin's conversation with Donna Thompson, he was on the phone with Pulaski PD. In less than thirty minutes four unmarked State Police cruisers and two village patrol cars converged on Clinton Street in the small village of Pulaski. Three officers walked around to the back of the house at 117 Clinton Street, with two officers on each side and three at the front door. The lead trooper radioed, "Everyone in position?"

"Ten-four," came the replies.

With the help of a battering ram, the front door flew open. Officers yelled "POLICE, NEW YORK STATE POLICE!" The troopers entered the residence, fanning out and checking each room. Rock-o Barns bolted out the back door and into the waiting muzzles of three M-16 assault rifles.

"ON THE GROUND, NOW!"

Ronnie Barns instantly threw himself flat on the ground with his face in the dirt. A second officer placed his knee in the center of Barns' back and put handcuffs on the suspect.

"What's this all about?" Barns yelled.

The trooper leaned over his shoulder and said quietly, "We just want to talk to you, Ronnie. We thank you for your cooperation," and escorted him to the cruiser.

They drove Ronnie Barns, aka Rock-o, to the substation in Pulaski and sat him down in Interrogation Room 1. "Will you take these cuffs off please?"

"The trooper said, "I'll take that under advisement," and left the room. He reopened the door and said, "Sorry, No!"

Thirty minutes later Detective Whallin entered the station. "Where is he?"

"He's waiting patiently in Room one Detective."

"Did you get anything with the search warrant?"

"Oh yeah! We have a roll of duct tape, same color that was used on Kellogg. Forensics will determine if it's the same batch. We have a black hood, which may have some of Kellogg's DNA inside. We also have a partial box of .22 caliber ammunition. Plus the description of the car you gave us is a match. Right down to the plate number and the dent in the driver's side rear door."

"Good job! Okay, here's what I'd like to do.............."

Detective Whallin entered Interrogation Room 1, shocked when walked in to see Ronnie Barns in hand cuffs. "TROOPER!"

"Sir?"

"What's this man doing in handcuffs? Get them off! I sent the order that I just wanted to talk to Mr. Barns!"

"Sorry sir, there must have been some misunderstanding." The trooper quickly took the handcuffs off Barns, "We're sorry for any inconvenience, Mr. Barns. Can I get you anything, coffee, soda, water?"

"Yeah, a Mountain Dew would be good, thanks."

"Right away, Mr. Barns, and again we apologize." The trooper left to get Rock-o a Mountain Dew.

Detective Whallin sat across from Ronnie Barns and placed a recorder in front of him. "I'd like to record this interview, if that's okay, Mr. Barns."

"Do I need a lawyer or anything?"

"I see no need for you to go to that bother, Mr. Barns. We're just looking for information."

A Mountain Dew was placed on the table in front of Ronnie. "Again Mr. Barns we apologize for the miss understanding." Ronnie looked up at the Trooper at the same instant he opened his Mountain Dew. "Don't worry about it. You were saying Detective?"

"I'm sure you've heard about the abduction in Adams a couple of nights ago."

"No, no I didn't hear about no abduction."

Whallin went on, "Yes, a young man about twenty-one years was taken from the Seven-Eleven shop in Adams."

"Oh, I'm real sorry to hear that. Is she okay?" Whallin smiled and thought to himself. *"That's once."*

"We're not sure, Mr. Barns. We haven't found him yet. Now we understand that you were in Adams that night and we are wondering if by any chance you may have seen anything out of place in the vicinity of the Seven-Eleven shop. Anything at all?"

Ronnie took a big drink from his soda. "Yeah, I was there! But I didn't see no girl being abducted or I would have done something to help her, you know! A young, small girl like that. I mean, you know, she can't defend herself. If I'd have been there, I'd a kicked some ass. You can bet on that."

*"That's twice, that's enough."*

Detective Whallin stood up with his hands still on the table.

*"Got ya!"*

"You were there, you son of a bitch. You, with your black Ford and your shaved head. We have the tape you used, the hood you put over her head and a box of .22 shells that you used to shoot the man that DID try to help that defenseless little girl." Whallin reached across the table and with his pen slid the Mountain Dew can to his side then yanked Barns' shirt sleeve up and saw the scratch marks on his arm. "And what do you bet that your DNA matches the DNA we found under that small little girl's finger nails. We also......."

At that point, another trooper came into the interrogation room and whispered in the detective's ear. "Thank you officer." Whallin now smiling from ear to ear. "And Barns."

"Yeah."

"You'd better get yourself a real good lawyer, because now we have the gun."

Whallin, already standing placed Ronnie Barns, AKA Rock-O under arrest for the kidnapping of Bonnie Kellogg and the Murder of Thomas Blake. After reading him his rights

Whallin left the room. Barns sat there banging his head on the table. Two troopers walked into the room and escorted Mr. Barns to lock up.

Detective Whallin asked to have all of the evidence sent over to forensics and requested a warrant for a cheek swab from Barns to confirm a DNA match to the material collected from the soda can and that witch was taken from Bonnie Kellogg's finger nails. "I hope we can get a ballistics match on the gun. And cross your fingers for a fingerprint or two."

Detective Whallin walked over to the phone and dialed Donna Thompson's number. Bob answered the phone. "Mr. Thompson, this is Detective Whallin."

"Yes, Detective?"

"I just wanted you to know that we have Barns in custody. The information your wife gave us led us straight to him. We recovered the gun, shells, duct tape used to restrain Ms. Kellogg, and the hood he placed over her head. I am confident that bail will be denied. He's going away for a good long time."

"That's good news detective. We'll rest a whole lot easier now, thanks to you and your team."

"The thanks belong to your wife and Tom Blake. Without their help, the case may never have been solved, Mr. Thompson. Please tell her I said so."

"I will, Detective. Good-bye."

Whallin then dialed the number for Bonnie Kellogg. "Hello. Bonnie?"

"No, this is her sister."

"This is Detective Whallin of the New York State Police."

"Yes detective?"

"I just wanted Bonnie to know that we have a suspect in custody. And that we are confident we have the right man. I am also confident that bail will be denied."

"Oh thank you, Detective," Bonnie's sister said gratefully. "You have just lifted a huge burden from our shoulders. Thank you. Oh, thank you so much!"

"Please tell your sister that by keeping a level head she managed to get some vital evidence, which will guarantee a conviction."

"I'll be sure and tell her." You could almost hear the smile on her face as she hung up the phone.

After Bob hung up the phone he turned to Donna. "It's over! They have him in custody. The detective is sure that bail will be denied. He also wanted me to be sure and thank you. Without you and Tom the case may have never been solved."

Donna's eyes began to fill. She wiped them dry and went to the kitchen. She placed her hand on the manila envelope.

Bob walked in. "It's over, Donna. Don't you think it's time you opened it?"

Donna picked up the envelope, held it close to her heart and closed her eyes. "Yes, Bob. I'm sure you're right."

She carefully opened the flap of the envelope and slid the contents out onto the counter. On top lay the cover letter.

*To whom it may concern;*

*This is my living trust. At the time that I am writing this my wife Annie has passed before me. We were never blessed with children and neither of us has any siblings. My father and both of Annie's parents are gone. My mother Rosemary is very frail and also may have little time left. I am appointing our closest friends, Robert and Donna Thompson, as executors of my estate.*

*All of my possessions are to be sold. Any and all debts I incurred are to be paid, along with my final expenses. After the executors' fee has been paid, all remaining assets are to be donated to the Black River Chapter of The Adirondack Mountain Club.*

*In return for my donation I ask only that two members of the chapter take my ashes and spread them in the same location that I spread my wife's ashes. The spot is located a short distance from the top of Mount Marcy. It is clearly marked on my GPS as waypoint 46s.*

*I want to thank you in advance for granting my final request.*

*Signed: Thomas Blake*

Donna finished reading the cover letter. She instantly turned around and fell into Bob's arms crying uncontrollably. Holding her tightly, Bob did his best to console her in her time of grief.

# Their Final Climb

## Chapter Fifteen

Donna called the Raymond Weldon Funeral home. A woman answered the phone. "Hello, Weldon Funeral Home. How may I help you?"

Hello. This is Donna Thompson. I would like to make the arrangements for Thomas Blake."

Mrs. Thompson, I'm so glad you called. We received a call that Mr. Blake's body was ready to be picked up, but we have no idea what is to be done."

"May my husband and I stop in, please?"

"Why yes, please come right over."

Raymond Weldon answered the door and the Thompsons walked in and sat in his office. He spoke softly, "First of all let me say that we are sorry for your loss."

"Thank you, Mr. Weldon," Donna replied.

"Was Mr. Blake a relative?"

Bob explained. "No, he and his wife were our neighbors and closest friends. They have no other family except Tom's mother and she is not well at all. When they told her of her son's passing she had a slight stroke that has left her incapacitated."

"I'm sorry to hear that."

Donna continued. "So you see, Mr. Weldon, we are all you have."

"Do you have any information about arrangements?"

"Yes, he spelled it all out for us. He wants to be cremated, with a very small service the same as his wife's, just three weeks ago."

"Yes, yes, I remember Mrs. Blake's service."

Donna went on, "He also wants someone from the Black River Chapter of The Adirondack Mountain Club to spread his ashes. We know no one in that club. We wonder if you do."

"As a matter of fact, I do. Their names are Mindy and Nathan Newert. I'm sure that you can find their number in the phone book." Donna jotted their names on a piece of paper.

"Is there anything else that you need Mr. Weldon?"

"No, I think that will cover it."

"Thank you very much."

"Mr. and Mrs. Thompson I'll give you a call with the details as soon as I've completed them."

Bob and Donna drove home, looked up the Newarts in the phone book, and dialed the number. Mindy answered the phone.

"Mrs. Newert?"

"Yes, this is Mrs. Newert. Can I help you?"

"I hope so. I really hope so. My name is Donna Thompson. Do you have a few minutes?"

"Yes, I'm not at all busy at the moment. What do you need?"

"Well, this may take a while. My neighbor's wife died three weeks ago. She was cremated and he took her ashes up to Mount Marcy and spread them there. Now he has died and he wants his ashes spread in the same spot. In his will, he wants all of his final expenses paid and after that the remainder of his estate is to be donated to your chapter of the ADK club. His only request was that two members of your club spread his ashes on the exact spot that he spread his wife's. Is that a possibility?"

"I don't know. It's an awfully big area. Do you have any idea where this spot is?"

"Yes, I think so. He said he has it marked on his GPS as Waypoint 46. Does that make sense to you?"

"Well yes, if he has it marked like that we can walk right to the spot."

Donna went on, "Is this anything we can ask two members of your club to do for us?"

"I'm sure that my husband and I would be happy to do that for you Donna."

"I'd like you to come to Tom's service, if you would. I'll give you his urn there. Is that agreeable to you?"

"Sure, just let me know where and when and we'll be there."

"Oh, thank you so much Mindy. I really do appreciate this. I will be in touch with final details."

"We'll be glad to help you out."

Raymond Weldon soon called Donna with the time and place for Tom's service and reception. "The service, Mrs. Thompson, will be here, the same as his wife's. The service will begin at two o'clock tomorrow and there will be a reception at the American Legion immediately following the service. The obituary is in tonight's paper."

"Thank you, Mr. Weldon."

"You're welcome, Mrs. Thompson."

Donna hung up the phone, turned to Bob. "I want your honest opinion, Bob. What do you think about you and me going along with Mindy and Nathan to spread Tom's ashes? I really feel that we should."

Bob put the paper down and looked at Donna. "I hadn't thought about it, but if that's what you want to do, we'll do it."

Donna picked up the phone and called Mindy Newert. "Hello, Mindy?"

"Yes?"

"This is Donna Thompson."

"Yes Donna. I read Mr. Blake's obituary in the paper. My husband and I will be there."

"Thank you, but that's not what I called about. I think we have a change of plans. My husband and I would like to go along with you and your husband to spread Tom's ashes."

Mindy thought for a few seconds before she answered, "That's not a problem, Donna, but this is no walk in the park!"

"It's not?"

"No it's not. Mount Marcy is the highest peak in New York State. We plan on leaving right after the reception and driving to the Park. We're going to rent a room there and get up very early in the morning. The hike is about seven and a half miles up the mountain, with an elevation change of over three thousand feet. With the return trip back down, we will hike over fifteen miles in one day. Now let me ask you this, Donna. Can you do that?"

"I thank you for your honesty Mindy, but I'll do it if it kills me."

Mindy laughed. "With all due respect, it just may. Without camping overnight we won't have any time to spare."

"I promise you, Mindy, we will not hold you up."

"I'll hold you to that. We'll see you tomorrow. Bye-bye."

After her conversation with Mindy, Donna said to her husband, "We need to go over to Tom's house, Bob, and see if we can find some hiking boots that will fit us. This will be a fifteen mile hike and we don't have any time to break in a pair of boots."

Donna found Tom's house keys and let herself and Bob into the garage, then went downstairs where the camping gear was stored. Bob located a day pack. "We'll need this. And here are a couple of water bottles."

"Are there any more water bottles Bob?"

"A few. Why?"

"We may need them."

"Here Donna, try these on." Annie's boots fit like a glove.

"I don't see anything for you, Bob."

"Look upstairs. Tom probably wore his to work." They found Tom's boots in the kitchen, just inside the door. Bob pulled one on and to his surprise, it fit. They locked the house back up and went home.

At the service for Tom, the local minister said a few words, followed by The Lord's Prayer. Bob and Donna sat in the front row. David Willard said a few words about Tom's character and his great work ethic. Ask him to do it and it got done right, every time. He sat behind Bob and Donna, along with all of his men. A few of Annie's co-workers were there to pay their respects. And neighbors from Horner Drive filled the room. Mindy and Nathan Newert sat in the back beside Lillie from the diner.

On display at the reception was a collage of pictures of Tom and Annie. Mindy and Nathan were taken aback by the collage. Donna joined them.

"They loved the outdoors, didn't they Donna?"

"Yes they did. They wanted to become Forty-Sixers."

"Oh, how far did they get?"

"They only had one peak left. They saved the highest for last, Mt. Marcy. That's why we have to take him there."

Mindy just looked at Donna. "I understand now. We'll make sure they make it."

Donna, smiling, placed her hand on Mindy's, "Thank you, Mindy."

After the reception Bob and Donna put tables away and swept the floor. They made plans for Mindy and Nathan to meet them at their house before they headed for the park. Bob put everything they would need in the day pack, while Donna packed a change of clothes in a suitcase.

When everyone was ready, Mindy and Nathan led the way into the Adirondack Park. They drove through Harrisville, Star, Cranberry, Tupper and Saranac Lakes, then into Lake Placid.

"We'll get a couple of rooms here, and some dinner. Tomorrow we need to hit the trail no later than five a.m. Are you good with that Bob?"

Donna ask, "What time do you want us at our car?"

"By 4:15a.m., okay?"

Bob looked to Donna. "We'll be here."

Both couples rented a room and took showers. By accident they ran into each other in the restaurant and had dinner together. They idly chatted about this and that. Donna and Bob told their guests about Tom and Annie -- what great friends and neighbors they were. Donna didn't mention the subject of talking with Tom to solve his murder. Before they left the restaurant, Bob ordered two club sandwiches to go for the hike tomorrow and took them to their room.

Next morning they met in the parking lot, as planned. "Just follow us to the trail head. It's about twenty minutes away," Mindy said. They got into their cars and left the parking lot.

Twenty minutes later they were pulling into Heart Lake. The sun was just beginning to light the sky. Everyone was dressed and ready to go. Nathan asked Bob what he had in the day pack.

"A couple of sandwiches, extra water, Tom's ashes, his GPS, and his log book."

"Why don't you give all that to me? I'll carry it. All I want you to do is walk, okay Bob?"

"Great. Thanks, Nathan."

Mindy signed in at the register and led the way. They walked for a couple of hours, then took their first break. "How are you holding up, Donna?"

"Its work, that's for sure, but I promise I won't hold you up." Mindy smiled. "Ready?"

Donna, back on her feet. "Let's go!"

They hiked past Marcy Dam and continued up. They stopped at Indian Falls and refilled their water bottles, then kept going. The summit came into sight. Nathan spoke up. "Mindy, let's take a break."

"Okay, What's up?"

"I want to start Tom's GPS and search for waypoint 46. We may be getting close. The summit is socked in with fog. I don't know how close we might be."

Donna sat on the ground for a second, then went flat on her back. Mindy walked over to her. "I told you this was no walk in the park. But I'll hand it to you, Donna. You're not holding us up."

"I had no idea it would be this hard Mindy. And all I have to do is walk!"

Nathan looked at the GPS. "According to this it's just under a mile away. It's one o'clock now. Would you like to eat your sandwich and take a short break?"

Bob looked to Donna then back to Nathan. "If that's what you want us to do, we'll do it."

Bob handed Donna her sandwich and asked about her water.

"I still have some. My god, Mindy, you're not even breathing hard."

Mindy smiled. "This is our second world, much as it was for Tom and Annie. Sounds that way anyway."

Nathan stood. "Time to go." They all stood and Mindy led the way. They walked up into the fog and had no view at all. They could only see about thirty yards. Nathan kept his eyes on the GPS. When they reached the east shoulder he said, "Stop! It looks like this could be the spot. Just let me walk around a bit." Nathan dropped his pack and everyone else took a seat.

"Yes, this is it, I'm sure. Right here on this shoulder."

Nathan took the urn from his pack and handed it to Bob. Donna stood and walked over to Bob's side. She turned to Nathan. "There's someone over there Nathan."

Nathan looked into the fog. "I'm surprised, No one passed us on the way up." He looked around. "Where? I don't see anyone."

Donna pointed. "Right over there." Mindy looked and shrugged her shoulders.

Bob opened the urn, looked at Donna. "Is there anything you want to say, hon?"

Donna paused, bowed her head. "This is just as you wanted, Tom. Rest in peace, here with Annie."

Just then Bob threw the ashes in a high, wide half circle. The person that Donna had seen started walking closer. "They're coming closer, Nathan."

"These peaks have summit stewards, people who try to protect the fragile vegetation on the summit. But I don't see anyone." Mindy stood by Nathan and shook her head and shrugged her shoulders.

Donna held Bob's arm as the image came closer through the fog. Bob leaned his head toward Donna. "What do you see? Tell me exactly what you see."

As the image came closer. "It's a woman. It's a young woman. She looks familiar." Donna stared into the fog and as if struck by a bolt of lightning Donna went ridged, gasped for air placing her right hand over her mouth. "IT'S THAT WOMAN, BOB! She's the one who gave Tom the kiss at Annie's reception. The one I saw at Tom's house for days afterward."

She walked straight toward them. Then, without even looking at them, she walked by.

"OH MY GOD, BOB. IT'S... IT'S ANNIE!" Donna watched her as she opened her arms and walked straight into the arms of ...TOM.

"Tell me, Donna. Tell me what you see."

"IT'S TOM. SHE'S HUGGING TOM! They're so young. They look exactly the way they looked when they bought the house, remember?" Bob nodded his head. "They're standing, looking at each other, holding each other's hands. Tom is asking her something."

"What's he asking her Donna. Can you hear him?"

Donna stared and softly said. "As clear as if I was holding the envelope."

"Are you ready Annie?"

"Annie is smiling and shaking her head yes. Now they've turned toward the summit, they're running, Bob, holding each other's hand and running toward the summit. Now they're at the top. Annie jumped into Tom's arms and locking her legs around his waist, she's hugging his neck. She's raising her arms high into the sky with clinched fists in triumph. Tom is spinning her around. They've done it, Bob. They ARE Forty-Sixers. The book, Bob. Where is the book?"

"Nathan, I need Tom's log." Nathan pulled it from his pack and handed it to Donna.

She opened it to the last page. Donna read the column, "PEAK ... 46, MOUNTAIN ...Mount Marcy, TIME ... it's 1:37 p.m., DATE ... July 6, WEATHER ... fog at the summit."

"Is that it Donna? Have they done it?"

"That's it, Bob. They are now officially Forty-Sixers." Donna looked back to the summit, waving Tom's log book high above her head. With their arms around each other Tom and Annie smiled back at Donna and waved.

"I hate to rush you two, but we still have a long way to go." Bob handed the log book back to Nathan and he put it in his day pack.

They were all ready to head back down when the fog lifted, the sky opened up to a beautiful blue, and bright sunshine. Donna turned around for just one more look and saw two young eagles soaring among the High Peaks .............. TOGETHER!